NICE PEOPLE ON PLANES

NICE PEOPLE ON PLANES

LANA HART

Copyright © 2025 by Lana Hart

ISBN 978-1-0670981-1-7 (pbk)
ISBN 978-1-0670981-0-0 (eBook)

All rights reserved. No part of this book may be reproduced, stored in a retrieval system, or transmitted in any form or by any means – electronic, mechanical, photocopying, recording, or otherwise – without prior written permission of the publisher, except in the case of brief quotations embodied in critical articles or reviews.

This is a work of fiction. Names, characters, places, and incidents are products of the author's imagination or are used fictitiously. Any resemblance to actual persons, living or dead, or actual events is purely coincidental.

Katima Publishing, New Zealand

Cover design: Cat Taylor
Front cover photo: Sasha Freemind on Unsplash
Back cover photo: Joyful on Unsplash

For Gemma

and her great great grandmother

Cora Shupe

A hidden connection is stronger than an obvious one

–Heraclitus

When did this begin?

Which passing comments of a stranger became something more than a whiling away of empty hours?

When did the words that tumbled out in that rare intimacy first take on a darker meaning?

Last year, I met an elegant Jordanian woman on a flight from Miami. A perfumer, travelling the world to design new fragrances for the superrich. Did we meet before or after this thing started?

Should my trickle of suspicion have come – in my messed-up head with too many hours alone in a cramped and hurried world – sooner? Or am I imagining ribbons of meaning in those conversations, weaving them together in ways which, at the time, did not yet exist?

If only the clouds could tell. They were there the whole time, plane after passing plane.

Chapter 1

LOS ANGELES – DENVER
DEPARTS 2:46 PM
FEB 21, 2022

Purposeful. Perky. He was lanky and poised. Another 'P' word to describe him? I looked out the window and considered this as he side-stepped into the middle seat, ignoring, as we do, the awkwardness of bodies rearranging, of unforgiving spaces.

Had he been one of them too?

That day, Black Sabbath is what I needed. To lose myself in their blasts of sinister poetry after that hectic week. But now a warm numbness pressed down, paralyzing my upper frame with its important attachments: arms, fingers. A baby behind me chortled. The plane jerked forward, its engines rising in pitch and volume. I let myself sink into those seconds of nature-defying power as the machine ran then sprinted then threw us into that first moment of lift.

Exhilarating, even after all these flights.

My hands found a rhythm, moving methodically as the plane levelled off. I reached for my purse.

The man next to me leaned over and looked out the window. "You can't beat LA from above," he said in what sounded like a radio voice, his morning program rousing us into the day.

"Much prettier than the real thing," I said, pulling my purse to my lap and letting my hand move inside. Soft felt. And the sharper edges of a lipstick case.

We sat for a moment taking in the zagging coastline against the linked-up suburbs, like two old people sitting on a park bench watching the children pass.

The plane veered east; the sea disappeared.

"Heading home?" he asked.

"Yep, been in LA for work. Heading to Chicago."

"Ahh … my kind of town," he smiled. My mom used to say if she got a penny every time we kids fought … same goes for strangers who act like Sinatra every time that place is mentioned.

"You? Going home?" I asked.

"Nope. Family. My dad's going into an old folks' home in Denver. Getting old." Then he added, as if he'd just thought of it, "Sad."

I turned slightly so I could get a look at him. Freshly shaven skin covering a thick jawline. Almost attractive in an electronics-store salesman sort of way.

"I'm sorry to hear that," I said, adding "but some of the aged care facilities these days are fabulous, aren't they?"

It's a funny thing that happens when two people sit together on a plane. Sometimes we ignore each other, even though we touch limbs, share air and the muted sounds of bodily functions. Our physical closeness is unusual – maybe that's why it can carry a greater force, one that can't be replicated at sea level. Except maybe on stuck elevators, say. We are, after all, soaring thousands of feet above the ground, in a vulnerable, adventurous thrust through space. Through time. Held together by the fact that we must do this almost unimaginable thing – move high above the earth at 500 miles per hour in a sealed container – alongside 300 other strangers.

Maybe it's this unspoken, shared understanding, masked by safety procedures and overly brewed coffees and the hypnotic hum of the engines, that makes people feel closer when they spend a couple of hours together, up there.

My new acquaintance moved further into this intimacy, tilting his head to reveal a substantial mole below his hairline.

"Not this one. Dad's broke," he said. "Can you believe it'll cost 700 bucks a week for a crappy nursing home? It's crazy. I had no idea before this all happened." The strong jaw bulged even further.

"Dad was a great saver," he continued, "always planned for his retirement like a squirrel. He and Mom split up when I was a kid, but there always seemed to be other women around after that."

I glimpsed out the window to see what the clouds were doing: cumulus, spotty convection clouds as the air heats on land, then rises. Nice.

I asked "Where did all his savings go? Did it get gobbled up after he retired?"

"Sort of," he said, shrugging his shoulders. "But mostly gobbled up by all his relationships. It was like, I don't know, like he could never just live on his own. First it was a lady with three kids, then an Indonesian nurse, then some lady from Oregon with a gambling problem. He seemed to lurch from marriage to marriage without thinking of the longer-term consequences. Every divorce meant less money in the bank, even after all that saving as a younger man."

I counted my own ex-husbands, envisioning a hyperbola graph to demonstrate their inverse proportionality; the number of marriages on one axis and my declining wealth on the other.

He talked about his father's Alzheimer's and the unnecessary treatments for things unrelated to the real problem. How it chewed through any cash reserves that his past wives hadn't.

"By the time he was finally diagnosed properly, he had $362 in the bank. He got Medicare-funded home help for a couple of months, but now…" he looked out my window, "now, he needs full-time care."

Paternal. That was another P-word. Can you feel paternal towards your own dad?

My neck was growing warmer despite the gloom of his story. Softer too. What had Sandra said? Imagine a warm gel sliding down your neck and shoulders, taking all that tension to the floor. I glanced at the carpet beneath my feet and wondered what that stress-imbued gel would look like, then told the man I was sorry to hear that.

"For me, though," and now he turned to face me, lining up that mole as if it were ready to take aim at my eye, "it's made me think long and hard about my retirement. Dad may've been a saver, but he never invested well. He never turned his assets into investments."

In that moment, I wondered if he could see into the spreadsheet of my own life with its unproductive marriages and crappy cars and kids that always seemed to keep my potential nest egg in check. I imagined the lines deepening on his forehead, financial advisor-like, as he poured over my 401k retirement fund, its inconsistent past aplomb on the page, and that jawline sharpening when my response to whether or not I have life insurance yields an alarming "no."

"If Dad had sold his assets instead of sitting on them, he'd be able to afford the decent care he deserves."

My fingers coiled themselves into a knot, like a clew of wriggling worms. All I could think of to say was, "What a shame."

"Anyway," he continued, relaxing a little, "that's why I'm heading to Denver. To put the old man away, I guess." He leaned his head back against the headrest, staring up at the air vent philosophically as the engines sang in a near-monotone.

I closed my eyes and yearned for Black Sabbath again, or something edgier. Instead, my own father appeared, tanned and cheerful. His knob-like bones sticking out on the tops of his shoulders and my using them as slippery handles when climbing on his back at Maroa beach. I could see the freckles beneath his tan, like fading constellations in the morning's first light. I felt his hands under my arms as he lifted me up high and threw me into the shallow sea, my squeals bouncing off the beach.

If he'd survived into old age, maybe he too would be staring out the window of some Oak Ridge old folks' home in a windswept town. I imagine him waiting for his lunch to be delivered to his room, and, since it hasn't come, he stands up, confused, letting his eyes wander to the button on the wall near the bed. He walks over and pushes it hard. He sits obediently, straight-backed, thinking about roast chicken with soft, bright vegetables. He focuses on his shoes to pass the time. There's a noise in the hall – it could be Brona – but then he realizes it's Mr. Dombosky trying to hit the nurses again. His stomach spins and he thinks of the beef stroganoff Brona used to make, succulent, rich sauce, like her thick hair and thick foreign accent.

Old Bert. The adage "you die as you lived" had never been truer. A short, sharp cardiac arrest while fishing. Quick and easy. At 68.

If Dad could see me now, what would he think of me in my corporate dress and unsensible shoes and streaks of blonde in my bobbed hair?

"I guess," the man's voice pulled me back to seat 16A, "it's a fairly typical situation these days."

"Do you visit him often?"

"Once or twice a year. But you know how it is – kids, jobs. Family holidays. You just start living your own life, I guess."

Philosophical? Partially.

"Yeah, and I'm sure that's what he would want," I said.

The view had transformed into a layer of thick, white fluff – everyday cumulus, nothing that interesting.

The plane shifted slightly. Engines dropped their pitch.

The short layover in Denver would give me enough time to fire off a few emails to Steve about my work at Drumme Manufacturing this week. He'll want to know the same two questions – how many billable hours and are there longer-term business opportunities – rather than the important stuff.

Like the foremen with their arms folded across their chests, shaking their heads at the Mexican staff. The lunchroom with its segregated tables of nationalities – Brazilians, Poles, Filipinos – like countries on a map divided by the lines of language. The boardroom, my pen running out of ink, crystal-ball-like, the moment I wrote "cultural differences" on the whiteboard, as if the pen itself knew it was unwise to even start. Drumme would keep me busy for a while: one-to-one leadership coaching, a management workshop, plus a staff session on cultural values for each division. It had been a hard, productive start this week, but I'd need to spend a lot more time in Los Angeles to carry the contract through.

Out my window, the foothills bulged with late-winter snow that spilled down to the plains. The expansiveness of Colorado suddenly made me feel hollowed, de-shelled. Without a center.

Or maybe it was the expectation of having to move through the crowded, solitary halls of yet another airport.

The plane lowered, growing the hills in size and power over me. I breathed through it. Two. Three.

"What a landing," the man said. He leaned over again to peer out the window. Covert mole revealed once more. "Almost didn't feel the wheels touch the ground."

"Mmmhmm!" I agreed in a voice that reminded me we'd once again become two strangers sharing an uncomfortably tiny bit of space. We waited quietly while a man of ambiguous ethnicity jostled in the overhead locker, resting his enormous forearm on the top of his seat as he waited to disembark.

"Well," I said, "it was nice talking to you. And I really do hope things turn out okay for your dad."

His focus was now fixed on the front of the plane. The line of passengers near the front started to ease; the cabin door must have been opened. He turned his head briefly and pressed his lips into a quick smile. "Thanks," he said. "I'm sure he'll be fine."

Pleased.

I pulled my body and my purse along the seats. A small plastic container had been left on the floor across the aisle. Two earplugs inside, one orange, one green. Why different colors?

I popped them in my bag. For later.

Chapter 2

*Upper North Island, New Zealand
Sunday, 23 October 2022*

Marilen held a friendly bunch of daffodils which she pushed towards me when I answered the door. She stood there, a walking garden in her floral dress and sunflower-yellow hat.

"Look at you!" I said, hugging her. "No one seems to age around here – you look exactly like I remember from last time."

Marilen let out her trademark deep-bellied laugh, brushing past me. Behind her floral veneer, she had an earthy, solid constitution. My grandma had had it too: Scottish background, wavy, slightly reddish hair, wide, firm cheekbones and shoulders that looked like they could do battle with extremely high winds.

"I see you've been busy," I said, nodding at the new curtains.

She squared her formidable form towards me, Celt-like. "Yes, well, they're not the prettiest petals in the garden," and there, that wonderful laugh again, "but they do the trick." She touched a hem. "The fabric was singed right the way through. Anyway, it was a good excuse to replace the old fellas – thank goodness all the tourists are finally coming back after Covid, eh?"

"Yes, thank goodness." The air that sank out of my chest brought a new insight: I'd been away from here too long.

*

That morning, I'd looked out the plane window to see brow-shaped crests of a thousand waves blinking at me, opened then shut, eyelids welcoming me to their coastline.

As a girl, I'd press my nose against the pane and call out "New Zealand!" to my family at my first glimpse of land. Christopher would follow my lead, shouting over and over at a volume greater than acceptable in the unwritten rules of aircraft cabins, forcing the older Carl to cover his face in embarrassment. Nearly 40 years later, I still had the urge to turn to the woman next to me and say *There it is!*

My approach to the North Island was different from those of every single one of my previous flights here. This time, I came from the west, from Australia, meeting the beaches west of Auckland and the wet-green forests of the Waitakere Ranges.

Long before the name "Aotearoa" started appearing on signs in New Zealand, my grandma had taught us to use it. "Land of the Long White Cloud," she'd explained as mine and Carl's eyes followed her long finger pointing up to the clouds above Maroa Bay. "Imagine being a sailor way way out at sea for months and finally coming across a bunch of clouds lined up in the distance. Land! Maybe it looked like a long white cloud from out there. But it was probably just a bunch of little cumulus ones like these," she'd giggled, looking up "– the sea air hitting land."

But as I approached Aotearoa from my own great distance, there wasn't a cloud in sight. My view of the canopy of the tropical forest, mottled with a million greens, was delightfully undisturbed.

The conference in Sydney that enabled this side trip to New Zealand had been full of experienced cultural practitioners and academics, with titles like Director of Ethnic and Anthropological Studies and Associate Professor of Business and Diversity.

At first, I'd felt out of place. Imposter. Inadequate. Impotent. The number of 'I' words to flail myself with at 2am had hit double digits.

To boost my confidence on Day 2, I'd reminded myself that I'd probably spent more time with people of ethnically diverse identities – and their employers – than three-quarters of the conference participants. Plus, they all knew I was a last-minute replacement speaker for Elise Madden, the Danish expert who'd recently taken the Hofstede material, rich with cultural values concepts in quantifiable measures, to its next, future-proofed stage. The conference organizers had thanked me graciously for delivering the presentation 'Cultural values training in American businesses: lessons and insights.' I tried not to imagine disappointment in their kind-sounding words. Irritant. Invader.

Steve would want to know if I'd picked up any new clients and how often I uttered those vital four words "Anderson and Bargh Ltd." I could probably follow up with a few new international contacts, to keep him happy.

But the conference had seemed a world away as I moved through the Auckland airport. Three years since I'd walked this well-worn path.

I'd always loved arriving. The free hot drinks offered by elderly volunteers, the soft chatter of the Kiwi accent as we waited for our luggage, even the drug-sniffing dog – who lingered near my bags a little longer than was comfortable – seemed casual and kind. I admired the Pacific genetic influence in the physical characteristics of the locals; the Customs Officer's lush eyebrows struck out from a face that looked as if its resting shape were set in observing children playing peacefully together. Through the arrival gates – bam! Suddenly in New Zealand.

Time for one of those strong flat whites. As I lined up with other fuzzy-eyed travelers, my gaze dropped to the airport floor. A scrunched-up receipt, a strip of soft plastic wrapping, nothing more.

I sat down to ready myself for the next stage of the journey, my fingers stroking the warm paper cup. A newborn baby was passed to her grandparents for the first time, the young mother draping her arm around her own mother's shoulders – a new branch of their family tree. Sprouted. A man wearing a sequined kurta broke into a sprint when he saw a woman waiting for him, her limbs extended as full and wide as a Texan sunset. Pasifika families burst through the opening in large groups to meet even larger groups of four-generation families, their parts merging into wholes, then disconnecting and reconnecting into different patterns. I drained the last of my coffee and pushed my hands towards the ceiling, spotting something on the floor that is shiny with light spots.

When I was young, my grandpa would arrange to have a car waiting for us at the airport. The car would've been borrowed from a friend who'd left the country for a couple of weeks or who'd been lucky enough to have a spare vehicle sitting in their driveway. Grandpa would ring my mom before we left America and tell her where the arranged car would be parked. Although the quality and size of the vehicle would always change – a rundown 7-seater minivan and a banana-yellow sportscar were two that I remembered – the location of the hidden key never did. When we spotted the car in the parking lot, Carl and I, with Christopher yanking on Mom's hand, *faster Momma faster*, would race to be the first one to fetch the key from above the back left tire.

These days, there was no one left to make such sensible arrangements.

My rental car moved smoothly through first, the sprawl of suburbs, then past smaller settlements, hosts to a gas station, pub, a few houses and a wooden primary school, its classrooms spilling onto wide decks and playing fields. At times I could have imagined I was in stretches of Louisiana or Kentucky, with the undulating hillsides and the groupings of cows dotting the landscapes. But then I'd see a sign – "Welcome to Mataporou" or "Karangaheke School"– and I knew where I was. Back in Aotearoa.

Trying hard to obey the KEEP LEFT signs, I grew distracted by the native trees, kissed with occasional crimson blooms, and by the playful creeks of the Coromandel Peninsula that spilled out from the roadside cliffs. After an hour of driving through the narrow, tarmacked road, I came to the sign I'd been looking for, its ageing font staying the test of time, its brown backing enduring the harsh seasons of sun and rain: Maroa Bay.

I turned right. The trees dipped further across the skinny road in an even moodier shade of green.

Sooner than expected, the winding shapes were interrupted by a bright rectangle, out of place amongst the curvaceous lines of nature. "EcoWorld Motel," it read, "Sustainable Seaside Accommodation."

Other shapes came into view – a freshly-asphalted street trimmed with squared-off plots that had been cleared of trees. A new sign instructing me to reduce my speed to 40 kilometers per hour (Grandpa would have laughed and said *stuff that*!). As I approached the settlement of Maroa Bay, I saw an entirely new subdivision that had been built since I'd last been here.

None of this should have surprised me. There'd been talk of "Auckland's newest playground" and properties being sold for urban, not rural, prices. Things were moving fast. Hopefully my mom's family's vacation house – "the bach" – would still feel remote and quiet.

On the main street, there was a new Indian restaurant with a takeaway window. An Italian gelato parlor had been built between the fish and chips shop and the rural grocery store. But the corner dairy – where, as kids, my brothers and I would get our daily ice creams and morning newspaper for our folks, where the milk came in glass bottles then later, big plastic ones – was exactly the same.

At the end of the main road was the small parking lot for the beach. On either side of it, thin dirt lanes gave access to the 20 or so beach houses. I turned left into it, noticing a new clearing. I honestly couldn't remember what had been there – other houses, sand dunes and scant bush, or had it always been a cleared lot?

The short stretch of sea-facing houses showed weatherboards peeling with paint. Threadbare curtains waved like flags in open windows. The six houses that were at "our end of the beach" appeared untouched by the gentrification of the rest of Maroa Bay.

At this stage of our long journey as children, Christopher would've been singing at the top of his lungs, *at the beach, Momma!* Later, with Tom, I'd be cajoling one of our kids, *we're here, look at the waves!* As the kids grew and husbands fled, I'd be asking them to switch off their phones and please look out the window. *Dylan - come on!*

I could hear their voices, all of them. Christopher's contagious laugh, the understated reassurance of Tom's words, the gasp of Dottie when, at age 4, she announced with confidence that she could see a sea monster out there, *can't you see it?*

It wasn't until I turned into the bumpy dirt driveway that I realized I had never been here alone. There were always other people to share this space with, to connect with. To keep my indulgences in check.

*

Marilen fondled the new curtains and chatted lovingly about the old house. As I watched her, another fact came driving home: in the past week, I hadn't been around anyone who'd known me for longer than a day. But Marilen had.

I asked, trying to stifle my sudden enthusiasm, "Would you have time for an early dinner with me at one of the local places? I see there's a couple new restaurants in town."

"True! Everything's getting bigger around here – including our choices of food," she beamed. "I'll swing by to pick you up around 5."

As she headed back to her car, I called out to her, "And thanks for the lovely daffodils!"

"All good, girl!" That laugh.

I waved and felt my shoulders shift downwards. The battle rhythm of Chicago life quietened. Fingers less busy. God it was good to be here again.

I fossicked around in the kitchen cabinets for a vase, but only found an empty screw-top jar, which worked fine for the flowers. I kicked off my shoes and headed up the beach as a low heaped cloud snuck in front of the sun, turning the golden sand into a darker honey.

"Cumulus humilis," my grandma would've said, her voice close as the cool sand squished between my toes. "Don't worry, mokopuna, Papatūāanuku is heating up, making a nice little cloud. It'll move on with the inland breeze."

*

Maroa Bay is protected from the incoming swell by its leeward angle and two long, pointed headlands, transforming the waves from powerful, C-shaped forces into knee-high, playful friends. It made for a quiet cove, attracting families with young children who could play safely on the sand, and older residents. If people wanted to surf or see expansive views, they could drive northwards up the peninsula.

The spring sun of the Southern Hemisphere felt hot on my skin. Young fathers stooped over their busy toddlers in loyal servitude, dogs commanded driftwood be thrown back into the sea, a teenage boy tried to ignore his younger sister emphatically burying his toes.

Several of the old houses towards the middle of the beach were in various states of hopeful renovation. Some had already been transformed into much larger and more modern dwellings, with floor-to-ceiling windows, expansive balconies and visible hot tubs. It was hard to call them 'baches' anymore; a couple new homes looked like they'd fit in along the Malibu waterfront or even Palm Beach. I wondered how much these houses were worth. I'd ask Marilen tonight.

Further down the beach, I was relieved to find the baches return to their ramshackle appearances, with makeshift crow's nests poking out of rooftops, windowed garages filled with messy bunks, and not-so-safe stairwells leaning against upstairs rooms for, I guessed, emergency midnight swims. Here were the New Zealand baches of my childhood.

A pull of wind lifted my hair behind my shoulders, washing me. Taking the grime of my long journey away. My back was sore from the flight and the drive from Auckland - it felt good to reach down to the sand to pick up a shimmering mussel shell. I examined it for a moment as I let my spine stretch towards the beach.

A strong splash of color in the distance turned my gaze. Bright orange. A light material waved at me against the backdrop of the sand and the weedy, patchy lawns of the baches. I picked up the shell and walked towards the color, expecting to find a towel or shirt that someone had forgotten. Instead, one end of a light scarf was buried shallowly in the sand, leaving the loose end to blow like a kite with each gust of onshore wind.

I released the fabric from the grip of the sand. Soft, creamy, it didn't belong on a beach. Silk. A woman's silk scarf. Someone would be missing this. I searched for a tag. Crepe de Chine – Alexander Wang. This was nice silk. A sea treasure of sorts. I shook it free of sand and tied it loosely around my neck.

In my hundreds of walks here, I'd always felt somewhat disappointed to get to this point. The sand gradually gave way to the dark rocks, the last bach's lawn eventuated into bush, and, instead of a bold and definitive ending, the beach merely petered out, steadily and naturally. Having to negotiate the tent-sized boulders, I would give up walking and turn around, somewhere.

This time, I stared at the ancient headland, admiring its solidity through not only space, but through time. As Da Vinci painted The Last Supper and languages and cultures stirred into the mix that would one day shape the European worldview, as the Crusades blended bloodlines and ideas across a vast area of the Middle East and Europe, and as the Minoans invented sewage systems, this headland had remained. Changed, of course, by earthquakes and hurricanes and the endless pounding of the Southern Ocean yet standing steadfast through the ages.

This idea felt good to me now, standing there taking in the vastness of it, pushing my more recent worries into a background hum.

I made a gentle curved pathway to pivot around a boulder. The idea came slowly at first, igniting, then simmering across the next few seconds.

That lady, the one from Taihang or somewhere in China. The orange silk scarf. The little boy - the story was surprisingly vivid to me now, as if I'd heard it yesterday instead of months before. Was good fortune on its way?

What a silly thought – those old stories have nothing to do with me.

I ran my thumb along the smoother surface inside the mussel shell. Of all the random things to find on a beach, a scarf … no. I'm not thinking those thoughts again.

But when the idea came back a second time, it hit me harder. All those arguments with Bryce. Spirituality and stories and the ancient pull of our ancestors.

I forced myself to focus on something else. The shell in my hand. I looked across the white-crested waves in the bay. Was the shellfish still attached to the headlands when I was learning to jump the waves here with Dad? Maybe it could've been a distant part of my childhood, here all along, growing under the surface of the sea as Carl and I snuck out to the Maroa Campground to hang out with the teens who taught me how to smoke, to kiss. Then, as Grandma passed my babies to Aunty Rose with the pride of a lioness, or as Tom deserted us, leaving us to ponder the strength of any of life's connections, the fish inside the shell died, fating it to float anchorless in the smoothing sea.

By the time I got back to the bach – noticing that, of Grandpa's two garage doors, one facing the road and the other facing the beach, the sea-facing one had formed new cracks and swatches of rust – I'd nearly forgotten about the scarf tied around my neck.

I removed it gently, as if handling it too roughly might draw out its supposed ancient curse. Then I folded it neatly on the kitchen bench.

I'd find a place, a very special place for it. Tomorrow.

*

Grandma and Grandpa had always had a no-frills approach to their bach. Although they'd lived in a comfortable house in Auckland, they'd never wanted their second home to be polished or fine. In fact, marks of honor were the unmatched kitchen chairs which Grandpa had collected from the discarded furniture that people left on the side of the road and the uncoordinated colors of the rooms which were beneficiaries of the leftover paint from the houses of their friends. The bach's shelves, linen and pots had served their purposes in previous lives before they'd found new jobs here.

When I first arrived earlier that day, I'd inspected each room in silence. Downstairs: the wobbly bunkbeds in the teenage bedroom, the little toilet which still leaned a bit to the left, the big bathroom where I'd helped Christopher wipe blood from the concrete floor so that Mom wouldn't stress about the cut on his foot. The door in the garage still creaked, like when we used to sneak out of it at night and Carl would shout-whisper *shut the fuck up!*

Everything was as it had been, since forever. Except for the curtains – I wasn't sure if the touch of new color gave the thick sofa and slightly-broken easy chair a bit of a lift or cast them by comparison into a duller light. Never mind.

Upstairs, I walked straight to the kitchen window, pulling back the curtains to reveal the most extraordinary view. Maroa beach – fine, golden sand, ancient yet always new – right there over the sink. Window by window, I let the sunlight in, throwing square blocks of light onto the thinning carpet.

There I was, chasing Carl through the kitchen with a plastic sand shovel, claiming he'd ruined my sand palace. There was Grandma, tanned, freckled hands pulling on my sunhat and patting sun block on my nose uttering "the New Zealand sun is so strong, Cora, you shan't get burned today." There's Mom, as I watched her from the window, admiring her bikinied beauty as she trotted to the shoreline, her calves firming into a curve with each step. In the background, I heard Dad yell at the charcoal on the barbie to stay lit.

Later, after Dad died and Mom stopped coming, we'd huddle around the kitchen table by candlelight telling made-up stories. We'd point our toes to the sky as we tried to float on our backs in the salty waves. Five o'clock, every day, rain or shine – we headed to the shoreline for drinks. Even if it was in raincoats and gumboots.

The corners of my mouth rose as I moved toward the bedrooms, that damp smell flooding me with fast, thick memories.

The old duvets and pillowcases had been replaced. Marilen had chosen well. But the rooms remained of a different era, when bedside tables and multi-socket power strips weren't required, when bedrooms were for sleeping and making love, not bingeing on Netflix or answering emails.

When I got to the final bedroom – "the backroom" – my breath changed. My chest, it flickered. The backroom was rarely used except for the largest groups of visitors due to its sunless position on the south side of the house. It was an odd-shaped room that had been added on, the story goes, when my mom and dad got married. Dad's family from Chicago was coming to stay, so Grandpa, a longtime do-it-yourselfer with a good set of carpentry skills and solid friends who could help, covered in the deck that extended out over the back of the garage, making yet another room to fill with mattresses and suitcases.

It worked. Despite Grandma complaining that the last coat of paint wasn't dry even as the guests from America arrived, the wedding was a smashing success with enough room for both families to stay together and celebrate. Bloodlines blended, I guess.

That was 1974. Now, the darkest room in the house was showing evidence of its long-time abandonment. The door was swollen from the damp and hard to open, the old mattresses thrown in a jumble in one corner, and the smell of mold was potent. Marilen had understandably not bothered to replace the curtains or the linen. Dampened by dust. Foliage of the forgotten. Mindful of mildew.

I looked at the closet door in the far corner of the room, camouflaged by neglect, instinctively pulling towards it.

Stop Cora. Not now. There are other things to do first.

*

A star anise floated in my curry. Marilen was only halfway through her glass of aromatic wine when I seemed to be ready for my next glass. We'd covered a range of topics – my family, her husband's latest fishing adventure, New Zealand's rebounding tourist sector. It was time to ask the question sitting, like a pesky dog wanting to be fed, at the top of my mind. That stupid scarf. I wouldn't be thinking about it again if I hadn't found that scarf.

"I heard a story a while back about Maroa beach, "I said hesitantly. "A terrible story really – and I wondered if you knew if it were true."

"Go on then."

"Ever heard of Dicky Bane?"

"Nope, who is he?"

"An early settler here, apparently. Connected to some massacre on the beach."

"Massacre?" she said on the other side of a mouthful. "Here at Maroa? I'd be surprised."

I could still see the man's face sitting next to me on the plane: dark, worried, twisted out of its natural position. There was no doubt that he believed that a massacre had happened here, long ago.

A car engine revved loudly up the main road from the beach. Diners turned their heads in unison towards the sound.

"Petrol heads," announced Marilen. "They're getting worse every year. Next thing you know they'll be gangs here!"

I let the heads of the people around us stop shaking back and forth before I tried again.

"It was a long time ago, like, when the whalers arrived here."

"Oh, way back then. No, I've never heard of anything like that before."

The knot of suspicion in my belly swelled. I hated that feeling, weighty, dark, untrusting, felt so many times in the past few months. Come on Cora, you're on vacation now. Send that old feeling away to a remote island off the coast of nowhere.

"I mean," she continued, "there were certainly lots of conflicts back in the day between Māori and the English and all. But I'd be surprised if there were an actual massacre like Parihaka or something. Why do you ask?"

"Nothing," I lied. "Hey, I noticed a lot more Māori language being used today at the airport than last time I was here. More signs and service people using it, stuff like that."

"True! It's like after a century of being told not to speak it, everyone is trying to use it again and, you know, help it survive. It was a dying language up until around the 1970s here."

"My grandma was into all that. She told us some of the old stories about creation and stuff and made us pronounce all the place names properly. Not an easy task for us Americans, I can assure you!"

Marilen widened her bright eyes and shared her belly laugh with the other diners. As her crescendo faded, she said "My mum always said your gran was such a lovely lady."

"Oh yeah, I'd forgotten they knew each other."

Marilen nodded, our eyes meeting. A new layer of connection.

"Sure did," she said. "There weren't that many Aucklanders out here back then. Mum knew everything and everyone that came and went from this place."

"Not surprised - who does *that* sound like?" I teased.

"These days," she giggled, chewed, then said, "there are just so many people in and out along the peninsula that you can't really keep up. And so many of the old settler families have moved on – moved into town or sold up altogether and left."

A spicy, simmering sensation in my chest had replaced the brick of distrust in my gut. I looked around at the other diners: sweating, sipping water, fanning themselves. I scooped up the last of my rice and chased it with the final sip of wine.

"Hey," said Marilen. "You see that sun dropping? I think we're in for a good one. How about we meander on down to the beach?"

When I stood up to leave, a deep tiredness set in. It had been a very long day, beginning in Sydney for the early morning flight. We walked, hips swaying loosely, Marilen chatting lightly about renting the bach out to a film crew during the Covid shutdown, replacing some of the crockery, and the development that had been happening in the area lately.

It was hard to take in everything she'd said. I kept thinking about the silk scarf and about Dicky Bane, trying to push away the slow, sickening doubt crawling up inside me. Thick sludge inhabiting spaces where better thoughts should go.

"... so there are lots of things for your family to think about. But I can see how knackered you are, Cora. There's a lot of fabulous sunsets on the Coromandel. Head off home now and I'll pop round tomorrow arvo with more info for you."

The road ended in the beach parking lot. People carried sandy pets and grumpy preschoolers, packing them into vehicles. We turned to look at the moon starting to rise on the horizon, egg-shaped, yellowed. I took in its unusual light.

"Yes, of course," I said. "Wait – information about what?"

"Let's go over it again tomorrow. Afternoon teatime, okay? I'll bring some of my homemade cheese scones."

"Thanks Marilen – sorry. I think I need to get some sleep now. Thank you for a lovely, lovely evening and for everything you do for our family. You've really kept it all going during this strange Covid time. My brothers and I really appreciate it."

We did that single cheek-kiss thing that Kiwis do, lightly patting each other's shoulders once. She turned back up the road towards her car. My steps toward the bach grew heavy and slow.

I watched the light below the moon sink into a pinky-orange soup shimmering above the sea. That, and the rolling quietness of the seas held me there for, well, I don't know how long.

When I finally pushed open the door to the bach, moonlight glittered in rectangle frames on the floors. Shimmers of light danced against the walls. I could see well enough to make my way up the stairs without turning on the lights. In the kitchen, the moon shone stronger, like a flashlight illuminating a cave. Right there, I slipped off my shoes and jeans, then walked a few steps towards the big bedroom. Everything else – hairclip, bra, make-up, shirt – I left on when I slipped into my grandparents' old bed.

The house, quiet as the smoothing sea. Me, alone.

Chapter 3

```
LOS ANGELES - CHICAGO
DEPARTS 9:05 AM
MARCH 15, 2022
```

One of the questions I regularly get in my cultural competency workshops is, "Is it OK to ask someone what country they're from?"

I have two answers. The short one goes like this: "I know it can be a socially awkward question to ask, like you want to box that person into a category or an ethnic profile. But I think it's all in the reason why you're asking it - the intention behind it. Are you curious about their ethnicity in a non-judgmental way, or are you bringing your unconscious bias into your assessment of the person? What's the context? Is it a reason to explore similarities or a reason to treat them differently? It depends on a lot of factors, but if you deliver the question with the idea of connecting, not separating, it's generally ok."

The longer one – and I have timed this to my seven-minute version, if time allows – brings in more flair and more research. I touch upon body language ("eyes wide open, leaning in with interest"), evolutionary processes ("an acknowledgement of the success of our species through ethnic diversification") and how conversations between strangers begin ("we all seek out points of connection – genetic connection is a touchpoint for our common humanness").

So, after the tidy, tiny woman sitting in 24B asked the classic opening line if I'd been visiting LA long or if I lived there, I turned away from watching the spikey cumulonimbus clouds and experimented with another version of that potentially awkward question.

"Just visiting. Work trip. I can hear from your accent that you probably weren't born in America. Is it China that you're from?"

She smiled graciously, revealing the hint of a gold cap on her upper premolar. In some cultures, a sign of wealth.

"Yes," her head bowed slightly, "I am from Taihang Mountains, on the border of Shanxi. Have you been to China?"

As she spoke, I couldn't help but wonder what her thoughts were on adapting to the different power-distance ratios of American and Chinese cultures. Maybe I could get a good anecdote for my training sessions, an example of how these differences are manifested in both countries. Something really timely. Fresh.

My fingers wriggled excitedly. Stop Cora. Just talk.

"Yes," I said, noticing and then trying to stop my over-articulation of each word. "I went to Beijing and Guangzhou as part of an Asian cultural study tour for my Master's. Ten, maybe twelve years ago - it must've changed a lot since then."

"It has changed a lot," she said, with patient spaces between each word. "So many people now. And you can no longer see the sun through the smog."

She was making impressive efforts at sounding monotone – not an easy task for native tonal language speakers, I'd read. I continued with my line of friendly questioning.

"Why did you come to America? Was it work?"

"As a student. Met my husband. Isn't that the way it usually is?" She arched a brow mischievously. I wasn't sure if she was poking fun at her compatriots or accusing me of negative stereotyping. I shook off my moment of paranoia with an innocent smile.

"A few years ago," I leaned my head her way, "I saw a performance group from your province, in Chicago. It was extraordinary: human-sized puppets and masked ballet dancers. I think there was even an erupting volcano on stage. I'd never seen anything like it."

"Yes, the mountain people of Taihang have ancient roots in puppetry and dance. But so do other regions in the north. There is a village near my birthplace which chooses babies for a life of performance, where they are trained from a very young age.

"There are many villages in my province that specialize in certain skills or qualities. There is an area that produces beautiful singers. That's where our famous Xi wan Di came from, whom you may know. Some towns have skilled jade carvers who have passed down their secrets for hundreds and even thousands of years. These traditions, as you may know, are hard for many Americans to fully appreciate."

I turned to look at her, catching another flash of gold as she shaped certain words. I was trying hard to listen to the meaning of the words but was also fascinated by her inflection. Her monotone sounded trained, formal. Elocution lessons?

"And then, there's the storytellers. From Guoliang, they take ancient stories and bring in lessons from the modern world. Proverbs about technology, for example, or people becoming too Western. These stories are created and told by the elders there and – if the messages are right – distributed by the Chinese government in the media."

"That's so interesting. I wonder – "

"My favorite story is the one they tell about a small boy who lived in the eastern mountains. He found a beautiful scarf made of the finest silk. It was bright orange – an unusual color in his land. He felt its softness and smelled its perfume and wanted to keep it for himself. He hid it under his sleeping mat at night, stroking it only when no one was watching. Suspecting it held some power over him, he finally confided in his mother, who instructed him to take the cloth immediately to the officials so they could return it to its owner."

She paused, allowing me to ask, "Did he?"

"Of course." One corner of her mouth pulled upwards. "He was an obedient child."

Her face grew animated and her voice strong. Its delivery sounded precise and practiced, as if she'd told the story many times before.

"Days passed and the boy's fingers still sought the magic and scent of the orange silk. Soon there came a knock on the door, it was a group of Chinese officials, who demanded to see the boy who had found the orange scarf. The frightened boy appeared at the door next to his mother."

Then her chin sharpened, and the corners of her mouth dropped.

"'Are you the boy who found this cloth?!' said the officials, as the child trembled at his mother's side.

"'I am,' said the boy. 'But I did not know whose it was and it pulled me to it, like hot rice.'

"The officials' faces turned soft and round. They laughed and said, 'It is the magic of the Qing dynasty. They wove the silk with the whiskers of the baku, a creature who eats dreams, and the scales of a longma, a winged horse. People are called to the cloth because it holds deep magic.' The mother pulled her son closer."

The woman was now leaning in close to me, her voice hushed with suspense. What a wonderful storyteller she was.

"Then, the officials said 'If a person who finds these cloths acts with good sense and integrity, they will be greatly rewarded. Their life will be filled with wealth, good fortune, and love. If they act with selfishness, their life will be plagued by nightmares and bad luck.'"

"Oh dear," I said, submitting myself to the story, not its logic.

She pulled away from me slightly and said in a lighter voice, "So, when I moved to America and sought a new life for myself, I still remembered the story of the orange silk and the fortune it can bring." Finally, the ends of her mouth pulled up in quiet satisfaction.

"Have you ever found one?"

"Not yet," she smiled – I couldn't tell if it was one of playfulness or sincerity. "But I know when I do," and here, that brow lifted again in an impressive curve, "if I act with good sense and integrity, it will bring me great fortune. The Guoliang storytellers are never wrong."

Her eyes pulled mine in for a moment, just a small one.

"And the boy? Did he and his family find their fortune?"

"Of course," she said, shrugging her shoulders lightly. "He lived a long and happy life with all the treasures he could ever imagine." She nodded definitively; the story was done.

I looked out at the hills of what I thought must be Oklahoma. The sun favored the west, spotlighting sides of hills and stretches of woodland on one side, forcing the eastern slopes to disappear into the shadows.

The pockets of cooler shades reminded me that I was heading to a colder place. A place where Christopher would be counting the days till summer.

When I saw him last week, my brother had been bundled up under a crocheted blanket in the community room, half-eaten chocolate muffin in hand. He'd shown his silly forced grin when he saw me, then tucked the blanket carefully around my legs after I sat down next to him.

"It's too much winter Cora," he'd said. "I want to go outside."

One of his new housemates, an older woman with Down Syndrome, laughed loudly from the couch next to us. "She's funny," he said with his usual spirit of acceptance as he shoved the remainder of the muffin into his mouth. He was right. March had been unusually wintery, and we were all ready to end the annual Chicago hibernation.

But working in LA for a few days had kickstarted my spring thaw. I wished I could bring some of that warmth home to Christopher.

I closed my eyes. A vivid, hot sun. I saw Tom on Maroa beach, his younger and less drunk version. With a long stick he drew rambling lines in the sand, as Dylan tottered along the stick's path. Dottie – just cresting beyond the infant stage – was hinged on Tom's hip in utter delight, her head bobbing in quick turns as her brother followed with delighted squeals.

I was there too. My younger self lying in the sand watching them, propped up on my elbows, sunhat perfectly shading my eyes. Does life get better than this?

Now, the woman's head next to me was slumped against the headrest, closed eyelids revealing a sage eyeshadow, every muscle in her face untensed.

I reached for my purse on the airplane floor, thrusting my hand deep into its contents. My fingers ran across a keyring I'd found yesterday. It was made of a heavy metal, maybe even silver, and shaped like a bucking horse. Without removing it from my bag, I ran my thumb along its unevenness. My eyelids dropped. Gave into the calm.

The plane's engine sang a meditative tune.

An orange silk scarf. Maybe I'd had a sort of magical scarf back then. A life of connections and meaning and ... so many treasures. Children, family, a shared future. The life Tom and I could've had with our two young kids.

I twisted my hips towards the plane window, hoping to shift that old, familiar sense of loneliness that sat centered above both hips. I stroked the keyring hard, then harder. When I opened my eyes again – were we above Illinois yet? – a thin tear of blood smeared across my thumb.

Chapter 4

```
CHICAGO - LOS ANGELES
   DEPARTS 8:27 AM
    APRIL 6, 2022
```

We tilted our heads down, following the person in front of us like school children in a fire drill. The woman in front of me had the squarish frame of an older woman, though her jeans seemed designed for a younger figure; a pouch of unfilled fabric hung under her hip bones. Maybe an old injury cocked her torso to the right – her neck and head tried to correct the asymmetry. I imagined her as a young woman, upright and true, unworn by the forces of the years, standing there in her blue denim jacket and Gloria Vanderbilt jeans. She was pretty back then, in a Midwestern sort of way, her pale skin flecked, her brown hair thick and rich with waves …

I stood up tall, forcing my own skeleton into a balanced state. Pulling up my pelvic floor. Hold one, two, three. Release two, three. Was my own body beginning its slow journey to one side, like a creek that turns to lower ground? Could these forces, ancient, natural and even ethnic as they might be, be re-routed?

The woman took a step forward, her box-like bottom moving the denim in small waves. I followed, visualizing what effect my own ass was having in my black jeans for the person standing behind me, in the unlikely event they were paying any attention to it at all.

I stepped onto the plane. Again. My fifth flight in less than two weeks. Stiff smile to the make-uped air hostess here. The usual shuffle of my carry-on bag there. Which window seat to LA this time?

Those problems with the Indian foreman at Drumme Manufacturing were thorny. Their largely Mexican workforce couldn't relate to the direct, prescriptive way in which their supervisors conveyed instructions or feedback. The supervisors were offended by the less formal attitude the workers had to their bosses. It was, as so many workplace problems are, a matter of culture, of hierarchy, of our default attitudes when under pressure or when facing conflict.

I could try the McKenzie technique – role playing, shoe-changing, empathy building – with the supervisors and hope that it would catch on with the wider group, but sub-continental attitudes towards workers lower down the social hierarchy were always slow to shift. I needed to think carefully about that. Maybe Hofstede's cultural onion model would be a better approach.

God, I needed some time at home. Time to get my kids together for more than a quick meal. To spend some time with both Dottie and Dylan and really pay attention to what's going on for them right now. Dylan and Janey seemed like they were getting serious, but I rarely saw them together for more than a rushed Sunday night. Dottie – my never-ending project – needed more from me than a phone call. Rolled-up sleeves, chai tea, life mapping on the kitchen table. My unkempt garden, those unanswered phone messages from life admin people, that one from overseas too. And Christopher. My Christopher.

I needed a week when I could visit him twice, for once. Mom and Dad would've expected this from me. They would've wanted this from me. Come on Cora.

Two weeks ago, when I'd swung by to drop off some brownies, I'd found him towering over a community house worker. She stood uncertainly underneath him as he pulled himself up to his full, intimidating height. I watched for a moment, unnoticed and ashamed in the foyer, to see how the altercation would unfold.

"You look at me and you think I'm stupid," he said in a breath that blasted down towards her chin. "Stop that. Stop thinking I'm stupid and let me go."

The compact woman, one I'd never met, held her ground with words. Her fingers wriggled in her pocket. Was she carrying an immobilizer?

"Christopher," she said calmly, "today is a stay-at-home day. In two more days, we'll take you out. Not today. Today we're playing games and watching tv. Do you want to watch 'Friends' with Marsha?"

Christopher was in no mood to negotiate. He was the same man as the boy I'd watched get so frustrated by what seemed to him to be continual limitations on his freedoms. "No," he would say to Mom as she'd tried to use reason to bring him back into line. "Stop bossing me! Go away."

"No," the grown man said. "There's nothing to do here. Stop bossing me and please go away right now!"

"Come on," the woman said comfortingly. She knew what she was doing. "Let's see if that Elvis documentary is still on Netflix. I know how much you love Elvis, Christopher. Let's ask Marsha if we can –"

"No! I don't want to watch TV. I want to go outside where the wind is!" he clenched his right fist and lifted it, shoulder-height, as if to strike the wall.

"Hi Christopher!" I spoke.

He looked towards me, taking a moment to re-adjust his focus. His face softened, just enough to assure me it would be ok.

"Cora, she won't let me go outside and its spring." He dropped his hand. "Why can't I go outside, Cora?"

Strings pulled my heart down to that place below my chest and above my stomach, where it often seemed to linger lately. My hand automatically rose to press against it, as if its warmth would send my heart up to its natural position again.

"You can!" I said with exaggerated cheerfulness. I turned to the woman and said, "if you don't mind, I'll sign him out for a short walk now."

The spell was broken. Christopher walked toward me and looked at me with his beautiful eyes: wide and brown, kind and hopeful, just like Dad's. I knew what my brother wanted to say if only he could find the right words. *Cora, I need a change, a big, important change in my life. This isn't enough for me.*

He hugged me lightly and said, "Brownies!" with his fat grin.

As we walked in the Chicago winds and talked about how to make cheesecake, I'd schemed about how we could afford a different day program or apply for some sort of education grant. Even though the trust that Mom and Dad had set up for his care was nearly depleted, Carl and I would have to find a way to top it up. And soon.

*

Row 24, window seat. I flipped open my laptop to check my morning emails: two client enquiries already today, a Polish neighborhood festival, a photo of Steve's birthday cake in the staff room, and some new research on cultural values out of the European Union. I downloaded the paper to read later.

I knew I should use the flight time to rest my overactive brain, to woolgather among the sparse clouds, to admire the sprinkling of little flat towns in Nebraska – towns where the train didn't stop anymore, where the tallest buildings were the silos, where people wondered what they'd do if the mill/mine/plant closed – before hitting the mountains out west.

But there was so much to think about and so much work to do. It was hard to shift down.

Dottie had refused to join Dylan and me for dinner on Sunday, claiming she had "a lot of stuff going on." That was code for slipping into mild depression and self-medicating with daily sessions of pot smoking. At first, I said what she'd want me to say: "All right, honey, take care. I love you." But after checking the roast chicken and poking the potatoes twice, I rang her back.

"I'm worried about you Dottie. We haven't had a decent talk for weeks. Is everything okay?"

"I'm fine. Just busy," she said in her well-practiced voice. But if I could see her now, she would have that slightly sunken, bluish look in the sockets of her eyes. Nothing to do with being annoyed. She couldn't lie to me anymore. I'd heard every one of those lines a hundred times.

"What have you been up to lately? How's the record shop?"

"Dunno. Not there anymore."

"What happened?"

"Mark's a jerk. Couldn't deal with him." My fingers gripped the phone.

"I'm sorry." As I uttered the next words, my lips – not for the first time with Dottie – operated independently from my brain.

Brain: how could you let that happen again why are you so unreliable are people really that bad that you can't seem to get along with them over and over again what did I do wrong if only your father were –

Lips: "I'm really sorry that it didn't work out. Mark seemed like such a nice guy."

"He's not. He kept complaining about me all the time. I'd had enough of the abuse."

I breathed deeply, quietly.

"Okay ... so have you got something else lined up?"

"No."

"What are you going to do?"

"Dunno."

Here it comes. The instinct. The uncontrollable instinct. To protect. To fix. For a moment, I thought I could be strong enough not to ask. But it came out. Like a belch.

"Do you need some money?"

"Maybe."

"When was your rent due?"

"Last week."

"Any other bills?"

"Electricity"

"How much?"

"My part is $50. Paul will pay the rest."

"Okay, I'll transfer some money now."

"Yep."

"Can we meet for lunch? I'm in town this week."

"For once."

"Dottie – did you just say, 'for once'?"

An audible sigh.

"Seriously Dottie, I can't help it if my work takes me away all the time. Besides, even if I were in town, you never seem to want to see me anyway. And Dylan."

"I gotta go Mom."

A warmth – no, a flush – rose up my neck. I needed to get out of this conversation too. "Okay, I'm going to text you on Wednesday and see if you feel like lunch. Kay?"

"Kay," she said curtly. Our phones disconnected, bomb-like.

I reached for the clutter of knick-knacks on the bedside table, my fingers finding the curve of a candle to run along.

Then I felt her, unborn, kicking inside me, shoving my bulge to one side as Tom and I looked on in fascination. Next, I saw her small face peering into our new kitten's eyes for the first time; two untamed creatures learning to negotiate a world of boundaries. I watched her take Dylan's hand as he led her through the school door, looking back at me once, then turning into her daring new world. I heard her call out for Tom after he moved out, her words *Daddy I'm scared* piercing the cold Chicago night with a sharpness and clarity that I hadn't expected. I watched the wind make her uncut hair dance behind her shoulders alongside her new stepbrothers as they kicked a soccer ball in the backyard; I leaned into their dad Simon and together we watched, soaking in our dreams of a new, blended family. A family that, only later, I realized she wanted nothing to do with.

This child, this dark, disaffected young woman, hadn't left our home with the confidence and abilities of her brother.

After dropping out of an IT course at junior college, Dottie had spent long periods in her sunless room gaming. I'd come home from work and suggest various ways to eject her from that space – a shared meal, a walk on the waterfront, a chat on the deck with Uncle Christopher or Dylan – but how do you move a 19-year-old from the thick pull of addiction?

One day, after I caused multiple interruptions to her online world, I stood in the doorway of her room. She marched towards me infuriated, accusing me of unforgivable breaches of privacy and independence. It was then that I noticed narrow, red lines on the inside of her forearm. Knife-lines.

The sight of them sent my heart thumping. At first, I imagined her papery skin splitting with a clean tear, blood soaking the bedspread, maybe even dripping onto the floor. But then – was it the slant of hallway light, or the look on her pale face? – I saw them for what they were: scars of rejection. Marks etched by years of feeling unloved and unwanted by the father she adored. How had I missed that when rejection was such a constant presence in my own life?

Getting Dottie to counselling sessions caused more fights than I cared to remember. After that, it was career counselling meetings, which ushered in a short stint at a chef school. A student loan meant she could finally afford to move into an apartment with other students, before she reported that cheffing was full of "misogynistic creeps who use passive aggressive mechanisms to get off on themselves."

The record store was next. God, I wished Tom was around to help me deal with this stuff. Raising two young kids alone was hard enough. But raising two young adults seemed even harder.

And drugs – they were everywhere in this town. Dottie had never been able to resist.

Why wasn't my love big enough to buoy her through the turbulence of these years? Maybe surviving her father's abandonment was all that she could do. Was it wrong for me to bring into her young life not one, but two more men who, like her father, ended up leaving us too?

I tried to remember when I first knew that things weren't as they should be with Dottie. The tantrums playing softball, even as her friends outgrew those outbursts. The phone calls from school – missing homework at first (maybe I should've monitored it better), then truancies. Dylan started calling her a "pothead" to her face, and one day in an argument, he yelled at me, "Everyone knows Dottie is the one at school that people get hash from – and you're too busy or blind to do anything about it!"

Busy. Blind. Bewildered. Bearing the weight of flying solo and years of making decisions about my kids on my own. Fucking Tom. I wondered what chilled out rehab clinic he was living in these days.

My friend Jess would say "just love her for who she is. Just show her that you're the one person who will always back her up. Some kids don't even have that."

But calls from the police at 3am and coming home from a work trip to find our townhouse trashed by her friends and reading my credit card statement (where had I left it?) with purchases at Liquor Mart in Englewood and a cash advance of

$400 … these had gradually put an end to my being the #1 back-up mom.

I reached for my purse. Ah, there it was. Soft, marshmallow-like. I squeezed it gently, letting the folds encircle my fingers. I drew the cloth up to my cheek, then under my nose, breathing in its subtle fumes.

There is more than one use for microfibers.

*

A soft wall of wind, an aftersmell, hit row 24 and brushed my face. Its scent was sweet, like petrichor. A large man with a large smile sat down next to me in the middle seat.

His interesting mix of physical features was a welcomed distraction from my circular thoughts: broad, light brown skin, dark hair and dark round eyes. What was his cultural and ethnic background – Sri Lankan? Pacific Islander? Possibly Filipino but with a mix of another genetic strand. Whatever it was, it was distantly familiar to me.

I watched the tops of altostratus clouds flatten into a smooth swerve after we took off. There must be high winds up here today.

Once the seatbelt light had clicked off and people started moving around the cabin, I began the conversation in the usual way. "Heading home to LA? Or have you been stuck in Chicago in our never-ending winter?"

His smile was natural, as if it was locked into his face like my safety belt clicked into its buckle. He nodded and smiled more, widely like his shoulders. "Heading back to the sun, thank goodness." The accent was broad, slightly British. After meeting my eyes for a second, he averted his gaze.

I was reminded of the Uono and Hietanen study, which found that the downward gaze deflection had strong correlations to culture, associated with not only personal space, but other significance. In Japan, for instance, direct eye contact represents aggression and confrontation. In Germany, it means engagement and connection. How our eyes meet or don't meet, it seems, play a starring role in the drama and meanings of our conversations.

The man continued to look to his knees as I spoke. Maybe he's from a more hierarchical culture where status characteristics – in my case, being older than him – count. Or maybe it's merely a personality trait. Maybe he's shy.

"Yeah, I've been in Chicago most of my life and even *I'm* ready to move after this winter. Were you visiting friends?"

"Yep." The wrinkles around his cheerful eyes were deep. "Just visiting. I've lived in LA since I was 16." The way he said his vowels was familiar, but with so few words yet spoken, I couldn't pin it down.

"So you weren't living in LA as a kid? Where did you grow up?"

"New Zealand."

Two words that felt like an electrical pulse moving from my chest to my toes. A connection. An almost genetic link on a plane high above a world that lacked connections to anywhere at all.

"My mom is Tongan," he continued, "and my dad was Māori. We have family in California, so we nipped over here to live closer to them."

"New Zealand Māori? How unusual. Not sure that I've met many Māori people in America."

"You might have. There are thousands of us in LA. A lot in San Fran too. But I guess most people think we're Mexican, so we get a bit, well, lost in the shuffle."

His shoulders jiggled as he laughed. His manner, an island feel. Like showing up a bit late or having your shirt untucked didn't matter. It drew me a bit closer, like an old friend.

"I guess they might mistake Māori for Mexican," I agreed. "My mom was from New Zealand. We had a lot of holidays there with her family."

"That right?! Most Americans don't even know where New Zealand is! I'm from the Coromandel Peninsula, east of Auckland."

"Really?! My mom's family – our family has a place – in Maroa, just south of Tairua."

"Maroa!" Now he turned his shoulders towards me. I twisted my torso towards him too. And there it was. The connection that my body needed. Random facts leading to something deeper, even if it was with a stranger.

"My family isn't far from there. In Tita Beach. You know it?"

I nodded. "My grandma took us there when we were little. Isn't there a big waterfall near the beach there?"

He dipped his head once.

"I've been there!" I said with an enthusiasm I hadn't felt in months. "It was so beautiful, but I remember being really scared too. My father's family would've *never* let me get that close to something so dangerous. I think I was, like, nine years old."

If the widest smiles could widen even further, his did, forming surprising new lines under his eyes. "You know Tita Beach! I've never met an American who's been to Tita Beach."

"We went there just once. We spent most of our time at the house in Maroa, but my grandma often took us to different places along the peninsula. You can hardly beat Maroa beach on a sunny day."

"Too right," he agreed, "It's a choice spot. When my older brother started driving, we'd pinch Mum's car and head out with our mates to Maroa. Got up to all sorts of trouble there!" His smile reshaped into a mischievous one and a vein in his neck popped out a little. He turned his head and asked, "Which end of the beach is your bach on?"

"North end, third bach from the end."

"Hmm. I'm surprised." He looked out thoughtfully through the window at the silky cirrus clouds lacing over, I think, eastern Iowa.

"Why?"

"Because there aren't many houses at that end of the beach. For good reason too."

"I suppose there's not. Ours is one of six at that end. The land sections are a bit bigger there, I guess."

"It's not that," he said. He held his gaze towards those clouds.

I tried to wait comfortably in the silence, like cultures unlike my own seem to do with such apparent ease.

His Adam's apple lowered, then rose again. "It's the stories about that end of the beach. Not many people will live there. Not after what happened there."

"What happened?"

"Maybe your grandparents didn't know. But I thought everyone from that area did. Or maybe it was just the Māori people that told those stories."

The sound of his voice made me feel warm and eager, drawing me closer to the fire of a possible story. I let my eyes ask him for more.

"You ever heard of Dicky Bane?"

I shook my head.

"He was a British whaler, came to Maroa in the mid 1800's. My people there loved him, he brought exotic things to trade, new spices, metal tools. He learned to speak a little of the local language and took a Māori wife. Lots of settlers did that. He was all good. They even gave him a Māori name: Tiki Pane.

The man took an exaggerated breath. "Then his mates started showing up. They were different from Dicky. Disrespectful, trying to overpower my people. They brought alcohol too. There were five or six guys who drank constantly, and one night," and here, he hushed his voice, "they attacked several of the local women. Once the Māori men heard about it, they went for the group of drunkards, but Dicky got in the way and stopped them from hurting his mates.

"The story goes that Dicky promised it would never happen again, and that he'd control his friends. They were traders, and my people were enjoying the new stuff that was coming in through these relationships. So the Māori men – pretty fierce warriors, you know –agreed to spare the lives of Dicky's friends. But just that once."

My mind drew upon postcard images of Māori warriors carrying carved wooden staffs, sharpened at one end.

"For a while, things seemed okay, and the area did well from the British and Māori trade. But then tensions started up again. The women lived in fear of the new settlers. Diseases started spreading – not only to their precious kumara crop, but to some of the babies in the tribe. The older boys grew envious of the white men's possessions and fought over the few bits of silver and muskets they'd traded."

I leaned my back against the wall of the plane so that I could watch him tell the story which, from the side, was growing more animated with each sentence.

"Dicky's wife, the beautiful Marama Tuipuni, was giving birth to their second child. It was a windy night, with Tangaroa, the Sea God, blowing angry waves at the shore of Maroa. Marama called out for Dicky in her labor, so he came to her. She cried, 'Your friends have brought evil to our village. This is your fault! What kind of place will your son have to grow up in with the bad spirits that now live here?' And then, at the top of her pains, she yelled, "How could you do this to my people?!'

"Her belly rolled with the moving child inside her, then she turned white, clutched Dicky's arms, and died. The baby did too. Drunk with rage and alcohol, Dicky returned to the beach where his friends were drinking and shot each and every one of them. Just shot 'em. Just like that. All of 'em."

The man paused dramatically before speaking again, now more hushed.

"They say Tangaroa sent massive waves that night to wash their bodies out to sea, but the evil spirits of the white settlers are locked in the place where they died. Right there on the north end of the beach."

I watched him nod his head slowly once, then twice.

"So that's why we never hung out there. Our parents wouldn't let us. They said Dicky Bane might get you if you went there, and that anyone who walked over the old spirits would be cursed by the diseases and addictions of Dicky's friends."

Now, the man looked directly at me. Unassumingly. Unashamed. Untouched.

I'd seen this before in many different nationalities. A belief that spiritual forces living among us – especially those captured in old legends and myths – could exert magnificent influence on our lives. I'd seen it in Mexican forestry workers who thought wood sprites were to blame for accidents, and Vietnamese workers who refused to enter worksites they thought were cursed, and Chinese managers who claimed that *mogwai* had infested factories where there was too much sexual promiscuity. These were the stories that had always helped decode the inexplicable forces around us, and that have made their way into America's workplaces and, therefore, into my own work.

I knew I should respond to the man with some reply to his extraordinary tale.

But my thoughts carried me to Maroa beach, digging my younger toes into the sand, feeling the strong Kiwi sun on my shoulders, the beginning of a glow that would later turn into an irritating burn.

The sand feels cool underneath. Protected from the intensity of the outside world. Then, it falls deeper under my toes, as if the seal of a vault has been pierced. It sucks sand downwards slowly at first, then the pace quickens. A narrow tunnel appears. I slide my toes into the opening, feeling its cool contrast to the hot sand above and letting my ankles, then knees drop into the gap. When my hips and shoulders slip beneath the surface of the beach, I find a secret room, a clandestine cupboard for the treasures I'd found on the beach or toys I'd discreetly stolen from my brother, my favorite drawings, and books I'd read. They're stacked on deep shelves of sand, in wild, un-uniformed rows, rambling like wildflowers through my private sand cave.

A warm calm moved to a space just below my heart. Then, remembering I was on United Airlines flight 667, I looked up and said brightly, "Well, I guess my grandparents hadn't heard that story when they decided to build a bach there." Hopefully that grin would return to the man's darkened face.

"I guess not," he said. "Or about the dozens of families that have lived there over the years. Cancers, alcoholism, one woman was driven mad by the cry of babies in the night."

"Well..." I searched for a noncommittal reply. "We've certainly had some lovely vacations there."

"Mmm," he muttered, but his face had not yet recovered from the shadows of the tale.

"So, where *did* you end up hanging out when you were kid? Did you go to other beaches?"

He didn't take my bait. "Aw, we hung out at the south end of Maroa beach a bit."

"Around the big boulders?"

"Yep, no worries there." And here his mouth drooped soberly again. "It's just the other end. We never went there."

It seemed a very sour turn in a conversation that'd started off with such a wonderful coincidence.

I couldn't shift my thinking about my family's idyllic holidays in that place as being poisoned by human blood. Part of me didn't really care – it was just a distant, old story.

But part of me did. How could all those people have died there without the tragedy being marked or shared in some official way, even if it was 150 years ago?

I turned our conversation towards my favorite New Zealand candy, what he missed the most about his native country, and some of the walks I'd taken my own children on near Tita Beach. His sentences were now more clipped. After the snack cart passed, I plugged in my headphones for some Led Zeppelin, feeling the urge for the tense vocals of *Immigrant Song*.

After a few riffs, Jess' parenting advice floated back to me. Maybe she's right. Maybe that's all Dottie really needs from me. She has an education, a few friends, and a mother who cares. A flawed, imperfect mother, but one that is with her all the way. Her back-up.

I must've nodded off. When I opened my eyes, the California desert was morphing into what looked like gigantic computer chips spread out, side by side. We'd hit the suburbs of LA.

The landing was jerky and noisy. The plane's wheels tottered wildly at first, making an uncomfortable roar. When the equilibrium and quiet was finally regained, I was left with a final question. In that long moment of expectation after the plane has stopped moving and before the cabin door is opened, I turned to the man and asked as nonchalantly as I could, "So whatever happened to Dicky Bane? Did he die too?"

Passengers stood and noisily gathered their items from the overhead lockers.

"Dead too. Shot himself that night," he said faintly, casting a brief glance my way.

"Sad story." I tried to pause long enough so as not to sound rude before saying, "Anyway, nice talking to you – neat to meet someone from New Zealand."

"You too," he said, and then, at last, that deep smile returned. "Bye," he said simply, stepping into the crawling line of passengers.

The legend of Dicky Bane. If only I could ask Mom or Grandma about it now. Had they heard it too?

Chapter 5

Maroa Bay
Monday, 24 October 2022

A pocket-sized tube of Australian hand cream. A worn deck of cards that I'd found in, of all places, a public restroom in San Francisco. An almost-complete set of coasters, each with a different image of Utah. That slender glass candle holder. I was impressed that I'd been able to pack that without its fragile base breaking.

The small plastic bottle of bubbles from the flight from New York back home where I saw a man that reminded me of Simon. The travel clock left behind in the hotel in Sydney. Bright ear plugs gathered on the way to Denver. So many things assembled on my way to Maroa Bay to add to my collection. And now, the silk scarf with its promises of good fortune.

Instinctively, I cast a glimpse over my shoulder before I allowed myself to touch them again. People have never understood my fascination with these treasures. Unpacking them, after they were so adoringly collected, admired, placed and travelled, had always been a task that I made sure I enjoyed alone.

The coasters had a smooth underside, as if someone had rubbed them against a rough table for many years, holding heavy mugs of beer or milk that hastened the erosion of any grip they may have started off with. My fingers ran along this frictionless surface, reminding me of Dottie's cheeks, which had once felt much the same against my hands.

I can't remember why I'd picked up a travel-sized bottle of insect repellent in Chicago's West End. There would've been a good reason for collecting it at the time. This one had a stylized picture of a tropical beach on the front. Maybe it reminded me of Maroa. Its lime green lettering looked so vibrant against the backdrop of Grandma's worn beige carpet. I stroked the fluorescent letters and felt the warmth move across my chest.

The fall of waves outside was becoming louder now. I remembered my grandma and Aunty Rose's warnings: *Get back from the water unless there's a big person around!*

The cards slipped through my fingers easily, like a professional dealer at a casino. I laid them on the carpet to inspect them more closely. The ace of hearts was in good shape, but the eight of diamonds had a small tear on its right corner. The soft pull from a child? Someone's foot ripping against it in a splay of cards on the floor? The next one was a three of spades, the hint of a brown liquid – coffee, maybe bourbon – near its center. Where had it been? What evidence of travel marked its cells? Were these permanent scars or removable blemishes? What pleasure had these things brought to others before bringing their pleasure to me?

I could hear my breath drawing in deeply as I stroked the shiny, spotted stone that I'd found on the floor at Auckland airport yesterday. There was a faint shimmer in its dark flecks when I held it up to catch the sunlight. My neck relaxed as I wondered where the stone came from originally and then - whose pocket had it dropped out of?

A sharp knock on the door stabbed through the calm air like fireworks on a still night. Without thinking, I frantically swept the items back into their cloth bag, pushing some under the couch. The knot I'd known all my life landed with a thud in my stomach: hard, guilty, embarrassed. By the time I sprinted down the stairs to the door, I was sweating.

"Goodness me Cora my love, you look like you've seen a bloody ghost! Are you ok?"

"Yes – sorry Marilen," I aimed for a quick recovery. "I had a big sleep in and I'm a bit tired from my time in Sydney. Please, come in."

"Nothing a scone and a cuppa won't fix - maybe a swim too. The water's warming up for summer already. Or is it warming up for global warming?" she big-laughed. "Either way, it'll help the jetlag."

Having been the bach's property manager for many years, Marilen needed no direction in that house. She headed straight across the rec room to the stairs. All I could think about was whether the bag under the upstairs couch was spilling across her line of sight as she marched through.

I followed her up, kicking a couple of the Utah coasters further under the couch as I passed behind her.

She unpacked her bulky bags, revealing a plate of cheese scones, a small tray holding a block of butter, and a manilla folder. We talked about the curry last night, the owners of the restaurant – a new migrant family that could only get permanent residence visas if they worked outside of Auckland – and the difficulties of bussing schoolchildren from the village into the nearest primary school.

"And then there's the high school!" she said. "Well, that's an entirely different kettle of fish. The poor sods need to go all the way to Tairua, an hour away, and then all the way back again. Imagine trying to arrange sleepovers with your mates who live that far away." Her idiosyncratic laugh softened the point considerably.

"There are literally hundreds of families like that around here," she continued. "The Council has been talking about building a new high school for decades but so far, it's all talk, no action. Anyway," she batted her complaints away with her hand and then used it to flip open the manilla file, "that's not why I'm here."

"Hey – can I make you a coffee? I could really use one right now," I said somewhat urgently.

"No thanks, but I'd love a tea. Did you see the milk in the fridge I left for you?"

That's right. 'White tea' as they call it. Strong, hot, with a dash of milk.

"Yes, thank you Marilen. Please, help yourself."

There are people in my life who move through the physical world with normal uncertainties and a healthy dose of curiosity. These people move carefully and are inclined to inspection and thought. They check things before deciding. They read labels. Jess, for example, hires babysitters or waits till Jack gets home from work so that she can do the family's grocery shopping with enough time to systematically read food labels and keep preservatives, food colorings and "other nasties" away from their children's digestive tracts. (This, she says, takes time and some strong reading glasses.)

Marilen wasn't one of these people. Simultaneously, she filled the electric kettle with water and clicked it on, pulled a coffee plunger from the cabinet and doused it with a level tablespoon of coffee, buttered the scones, and miracled a teabag from the far reaches of the pantry cupboard, together with two mugs. This, while she rattled off three more reasons why the area needs a high school. Her command of my family bach's kitchen was convincing.

" – and these new subdivisions are popping up all over the Coromandel. Did you see the developments when you drove into town yesterday?"

"Yeah, it took me by surprise. They're pretty big lots, aren't they?"

"They are, but I'm glad people have a bit of a garden to muck around in. They're making way for the mini mansions you probably saw on the beachfront. As I was saying last night, there's talk of a hotel going up in that vacant lot near the beach parking lot. They're waiting for a resource consent."

"What's that?"

"Permission from all the other stakeholders like landowners, the regional council, iwi – that's the Māori tribal groups. The law says that unless most of the stakeholders agree, the development can't go ahead."

"Makes sense. A big development like that would affect so many."

"True, especially us locals. Imagine dealing with all the tourists and staff for a big hotel here. Maroa just isn't set up for it. We don't have the roads and schools, and the sewage systems weren't built for thousands of people to shit in – pardon my French!"

The coffee Marilen had made me was starting to sharpen my thoughts. I visualized a hotel erupting from the beach parking lot like a fist thrust high in the air, teeming with pink-skinned tourists who'd ignored warnings about the intensity of the New Zealand sun.

"Anyway," she continued, "some guy from one of those posh Auckland firms rang me about three weeks ago and asked me to 'tease out' whether you'd want to sell this bach. I explained that it'd been in your family since forever and that it was owned by a family trust."

I tried to keep up with her fast chatter in an accent I hadn't yet fully adjusted to, but her next words had, importantly, more spaces between them.

"And then he said the weirdest thing, Cora. It bloody creeped me out, to be honest." Now, she put down her mug and flattened her hand on the old Formica table, her large breasts pressing into its edge.

"What?"

"He said yeah, but you, Cora, *you* are the legal guardian of one of your brothers, so the decision is really up to you."

A spark shot up my spine.

"Wait - like he knew about Christopher?"

"Yeah." Marilen nodded her head slowly, spookily.

"Is that like, on some official document tied to this property or something? Like on a trust deed or property title in this country?

"No." Her head moved from side to side.

"That's creepy all right. Where did this guy say he was from?"

"Huia Limited. Says he's working with developers from this area. I googled it but there's nothing there, except 20 other companies in New Zealand with 'huia' as part of their name. They're all like publishers or winemakers or honey farms, nothing about property."

"Maybe he just did a profile search on me and found something in my distant past about fundraising for Blueberry Hill, where Christopher lives."

"Maybe. Anyway, I said to this guy that I'd raise it with you and – since I'm just a property manager and nothing more – that you'd be in touch with him directly if you were interested in selling."

"Great."

"Well, about an hour later, I get this email which is, as far as I can tell, an actual offer to buy your property. I replied with a reminder that I wasn't a real estate agent, but that as courtesy to you, my client, I'd print out the offer and bring it to you when you visited this week."

She pushed the manilla folder across the table and said "Here it is but Cora, don't get too excited, it doesn't have a negotiating price on it. It just says 'to be confirmed' for the starting price, which is really weird. It's like they don't really know what level to start at, but they do know they want to buy the property, so they wanted to get something on paper. I guess."

I opened it hesitantly, as if something inside might jump out and grab me.

"I mentioned it to a real estate agent friend of mine, and she said that it's rare to see something like this, but every once in a while, you get a sale and purchase agreement with no asking price for, say, high-end or unique properties. She said it's kind of like an invitation to engage. Like foreplay, without the real deal," she snorted.

Marilen leaned back in the chair as I scanned the typed agreement. Looked like a normal offer to buy to me, with some New Zealand terms thrown in that I didn't really understand. But with no offer price, it was hard to know what to make of it.

I looked up at Marilen, who was now admiring the sky above the beach through the window, already forgetting the spooks of moments before.

"Looks like a good time for a swim if you're quick," she lilted.

I read the words in the file again, turning over in my mind how Huia Ltd may've found out that our family trust had been set up. When I looked up, there was a hole in the layer of lumpy stratocumulus clouds where bright rays shone through it, heaven-like, onto the entire length of the beach. At the two headlands, the light abruptly ended, as if the headlands were bookends, or entrances to a dark room that lay beyond.

"Oh look at that," I said, happy for the distraction. "The sun's come out at just the right time."

I can't pretend I didn't think about selling the bach as I dove into the cold waves that afternoon. I'd never thought about it before, but if somebody had gone so far as to research its owners, it must be worth a bit. How much, I wondered. If it were more than a million, maybe we could get some better care for Christopher and allow him to stretch out a little, become more independent. Or at least thrive in some other way, rather than sitting around watching tv all day.

But as the salt of a thousand ages washed over me, as my pores filled with water that had once jetted out of the pressure of clouds, and as my hair pulled with the weight of forces much larger than myself, I didn't care, for that moment, about any of it.

I swam, and let the magic of Maroa Bay seep in.

*

Finally, it was time. My cold wet hair would have to air dry. I let my swimming suit fall on the bedroom floor and pulled a long T-shirt over my head. That deep, familiar excitement pressed against the insides of my stomach as I took the key from the little zip in my cosmetic bag. I walked into the backroom, closing, through habit, the door quietly behind me. Even though no one, this time, was there.

The undersized door in the corner could've easily been mistaken for part of the wall in the dim light that snuck in around the edges of the ill-fitted curtains. Surely those curtains had been made for a smaller window.

The key fits cleanly into the lock, even after all these years. The door unlatches with a satisfying click. As I push the door open, I remember that the hinges squeak. They always have. Like the scratch of a match for a smoker, the click of the dice for a gambler, this works like a Pavlovian response.

Three years since the door opened. Spores and dust lift with a rush of new air; moisture finally fanned dry. I smell musk and plastic and something else, nearly forgotten. Then ... old sweat. A hint of lust.

I step in, letting the natural light play upon the surfaces. Ah, the defaced doll I'd quickly tucked into my towel so Carl wouldn't see, some 30 years ago. Now I smooth my fingers across her arms and scrunch her amber hair. Next to the doll is a small bible, almost-red leather still fighting against the fading of time. From a motel room in Tulsa – I was tired to the core, overwhelmed by the life I'd found myself in, needing to gather something for myself. I move my finger across the cover, carving a 'B' in the thin layer of dust. There they are – a mesh bag holding three marbles, the bright balls found near a drain on Chicago's Near North side. It had been sunny and warm that day, but for some reason I'd felt so alone in the world. As I'd bent down to pick them up, I'd suddenly felt content, a relief that the marbles were still a trio, a hope that they'd remain connected by time, by color, by having made the same journey to this place.

I flick on the switch. Light lands on the surfaces of the treasures in the narrow hall. The thin shelves lining both walls spill over with memories. At eye level, cardboard packaging from a neighbor's gift after Mom died – there was something about the way the pastel colors eased my grief that day. At knee level, small shells in plastic cups, their bottoms layered with sand collected in my childhood.

I step forward, trying to avoid crushing objects underfoot or to knock the clusters of treasures from the shelves. The smell of dust and history is stronger now, tickling the back of my throat. Ice cream wrappers from last century, empty bottles, the wads of yarn and thread ... I don't disturb them, but my shoulders and hips brush some to the floor with a quiet percussion.

It is here, in this most private of spaces, that I've always felt safe. As an adolescent, this room was an escape from two annoying brothers or new demands from a complicated world. In this room on the other side of the world, people can't judge me or expect things of me. Here, there is no Christopher, no rejection, no deadlines. I can organize then re-organize my treasures, putting things from the sea over there, human-made things over here. Then, I can group the blue things together, then the shades of orange and green, each object bringing me something visceral. Something real.

Here's a place that is now, and has always been, entirely my own.

Another step towards the darker end of the first passageway. Towards the shadows. Towards the place where I am utterly, and at last, connected.

Chapter 6

```
CHICAGO - MIAMI
DEPARTS 7:35 AM
MAY 3, 2022
```

The steely Chicago sky was a single color, a dull backdrop to our even duller movements. We tipped our foreheads to the ground, trying to ignore the push of the wintery wind that had come without warning, even as we expected May to deliver more hopeful days.

The man at the bus stop looking longingly down Clark Avenue for the heated bus to arrive, the pull of his face asking himself, "wasn't my life meant to be different than this?" A young woman with violet hair and a nose ring drew her hood up around her spikes, the angry expression in her eyes questioning, I imagined, her job, her latest fling, and why she just couldn't lose those extra pounds around her waist. A woman in heels and a business suit pushed a stroller along the crowded sidewalk, stopping to tuck a blanket more firmly around a squealing child. No one had ever explained to her, before, how hard this would be, how little of herself would be left within the filled-up hours of motherhood's everydays.

Everyone seemed as if they were looking for something else. Something more.

I'd watched them all as the taxi zigzagged up to I-94, the back of my head resting on the window frame. I sat up straighter when we finally sped up on the Interstate, but the rectangular buildings with their mirrored windows reflecting cars and concrete passageways did little to cheer me up.

The taxi driver said nothing at all, leaving me to soak in my own gloom, just like the day. And soak I did. Worries, like ivy, climbed up from below, encircling me. Maybe I should intervene in Dottie's life. Maybe it was time to get her over the line on seeing a psychologist or even just a life coach. Maybe it was the curse of Dicky Bane that she carried, and we needed an exorcist or something. Ha. And my kitchen, my fucking broken down old kitchen. This morning the tap on the sink vibrated angrily when I used it. A new crack was starting to appear in the countertop.

And then, there was this darker, deeper part of me that yearned to be filled up, to connect with things, or someone. Something that meant something … more.

As airplanes pointing their noses to O'Hare came into view, I realized that those buildings weren't just reflecting a sea of miserable people. They reflected my own emptiness.

I tried to smile at the puffed and primed flight attendants as they welcomed me on board. They were just doing their jobs, looking their part – why should I be so annoyed at their overpowering perfume? I took my window seat robotically, bag there, water bottle out, adjust jacket, click the buckle, deep breath.

Maybe the clouds, ironically, plus some Van Halen would brighten my day.

They were nimbostratus at first, with flat undersides forcing a grey hue over Greater Chicago. But by the time we crossed over the Illinois River, they were turning into cumulus castellatus. "A floating castle Cora, look!" Grandma would say, pointing out the kitchen window at Maroa Bay. "See how the castellatus is being pushed up from the cloud below it?"

The massive, bulging outcrops above Illinois were being pushed up too, causing impressive towers to form. The plane finally pierced one, instantly turning the sky from blue to a gluey grey, trillions of tiny water droplets latching onto the outside of the plane.

The outside layer of my window beaded with precipitation. My eyes followed a single fetus-shaped drop of water as it was pulled to the back of the plane by the thrust of the jets. If that drop could see inside – what would it see?

Christopher was so bored at Blueberry Hill. I needed to take him to my place more often, where there are people, and puzzles, and stories to talk about. He could only handle social occasions for a couple of hours before he became unsettled, but if we went for a family walk or made dessert together in my kitchen, he could last a bit longer.

Sunday night, family dinner night, is the one night when he insists on being at the community home. He loves the shared dinners hosted by the Rotary Clubs and Methodist churches of north Chicago. A couple of weeks ago, he told me he sat next to an old lady who had 12 kids - two sets of twins - and every single one of them, with their own kids, came together for Thanksgiving each year. Now that would've brought an adoring smile to my brother's face.

But the self-directed approach at Blueberry Hill – two meals a day, Bingo or a movie in the community room at 2pm, an outing every Saturday – these weren't quite enough to keep him doing much of anything. Except getting by. He, like me, needed something more.

I cranked up the volume. Van Halen's first album *Eruption*, dizzying, pulsing, especially alongside cumulus castellatus.

And it eased my guilt over having avoided admitting that I wasn't ready for my next work assignment. A conflict between different groups of managers, something about poor communication and maybe bullying. I wondered if Erin Meyer from the business school INSEAD has measured these differences. God Cora, get yourself organized. That should've been done three days ago.

Yet another mistake was that I should've gone to the bathroom before I boarded. I asked both the men next to me to please excuse me and watched them politely stand to let me by. It felt good to stride out after being shaped like a parenthesis for an hour. I tried to savor the movement of my feet, enjoy the clean click of the toilet door handle, and feel the warm water envelop my hands as I washed them.

It didn't help. I still felt blue.

Both men very stiffly let me back into the window seat, politely averting their eyes like doormen on Michigan Avenue, waiting for the next pretentious guest to greet.

"Thanks," I said with a smile, trying not to overdo it by flashing what Jess would call my "ready to talk" expression.

I must've failed. After we settled back into our seats, the bespectacled man next to me pointed to my phone and said, "I see you're a Van Halen fan."

"Yeah," I said. Not now.

"I saw them in Cincinnati on their last tour," he said, his head turned towards me slightly. "They hadn't lost that spark, I'll tell you that."

"Amazing all right."

"You should've seen the crowd," he continued. "The average age was probably, like, 60, with lots of older people looking like their titanium hips weren't cooperating."

Okay, small talk over, could I just get back to my self-pity and procrastination please? Three failed relationships, a directionless daughter, a crumbling old house … the rest of my days living as an old, lonely lady looking out the window of her life and reflecting on where the mistakes were, what she should've done.

I tried not to say anything to provoke conversation. I really did.

But after a few awkward seconds, it felt too dismissive not to say, "That must've been cool to be there."

"Cool is an understatement. It was one of the top three musical experiences of my life. One of my patients said they saw David Lee Roth eating at an outdoor café in LA, and he had makeup on. Not the stage makeup that you'd expect in a concert, but real eyeliner and – what's it called?" He ran his two index fingers along both cheekbones and pursed his lips.

"Blush?"

"Yeah, blush. My patient said he looked ridiculous!" he laughed.

I smiled, then turned my head to examine a corkscrewing cumulus nimbus.

"Did you hear there's a tribute band starting to tour?" he said. "November, apparently."

"Oh yeah?"

"Yeah." I'm sure he sensed my wanting to end the conversation. Why did I feel guilty about that? He's just some geeky doctor with the same taste in music as me.

He changed the subject. "So, are you from Chicago?"

"Yep."

"Love it there. My kinda town." Another penny for the jar.

"Hmm." I nodded slightly in agreement.

I started to reach for my earbuds. Then he said, "I'm an adolescent psychologist in Miami. Just went to a conference at McCormick Place. They sure know how to do conferences there."

His patients are teens. It piqued my interest enough to say, "Interesting job. Lots of emo teens giving in to the self-harming craze?"

He laughed, "Some of those. But the conference was about grief. How age affects how we deal with it. It's amazing, you know, what science is now telling us about the adolescent brain - the changes that occur in the brain due to grief can be so much more severe than the same episode in the adult brain."

He now had my full attention. Darn it.

He read my face accurately this time, continuing. "We're just starting to see some of these visible effects in the brain matter – the amygdala – especially if it's associated with trauma. So -"

"Hang on, what's the amygdala do again?"

"If only there were a simple answer for that – part of our lizard brains, handles survival instincts like fight or flight, and memories we need to stay alive. It does a lot more but – "

"Got it, go on."

He sat up straight, his excitement building. "Ok so, if adolescent and young adult grief alters neurobiological mechanisms, like, say, executive functions in the frontal lobe and - and the salience network and other functions, then the stress response isn't mediated as it is in brains not affected by grief – sorry if I'm sounding like a geek shrink but I – "

"No, go on!"

"So, these changes show structural vulnerabilities for developing psychological disorders and anxiety-related problems – if they're left unresolved – in adulthood."

I was glad to have taken that Psychology 101 class back in college. Even though this guy sounded like he was giving a psychology lecture, I actually knew what he was talking about. Sort of.

He continued. "All these findings which look at where the grief is affecting the brain give us stronger tools to address the damage caused by it."

"What can we do about it? I mean, if it's changed the brain itself, how can we unchange it?"

"Sort of like scars on your skin fading over time, the physical biomarkers caused by grief are showing signs of reversibility. The human brain can be re-wired through cognitive behavioral and other therapies – its malleability is able to change the very size and shape of the brain."

"So that's where you come in? With the therapy?"

"Yep. I'm a big fan of CBT. I use it on teens all the time. So for me, it's great to see hard evidence – brain scans, pathophysiological research – that it's working."

"Neat" I said, noting his abrupt departure from the lecture-stand voice to the everyday-man voice.

"I mean, we all have stuff from the past that we carry around with us: grief, loss, maybe trauma. And sometimes it feels like it may never go away, like a lifelong scar. But now we know that with the proper treatment, most old traumas can be healed and the behavior associated with it changed. The bad habits, the addictions, the messy relationships, the messy houses … all those disorders that may be caused by historical grief are now known to be neurologically fixable."

I wanted to say: what the hell do messy houses have to do with it?! I heard myself say, "That's good news."

"So, I help my patients by working with them to let go of the past, teaching them how to accept what happened, then move on, even give away items that represent the loss. Re-organize their rooms, for example, or take a new class at school, change social groups … these act as circuit breakers for the patterns of grief-related dysfunction and enable the brain to put down different neurological pathways that can lead to a full recovery."

"Hmm" I said, trying to think of more affirming words other than 'cool.' In that moment, I imagined my scarred-up brain as a map with hundreds of wriggling roads, all leading towards a large X, marked "Full Recovery."

He continued persistently, with the grace of a freight train. "For adults, it's letting go of links to the past: jobs, relationships and even houses can be loaded with reminders of the grief. The fresh start is liberating and sets in motion – with good therapy of course – the beginning of the physiological repair, the actual *tissue* damage in the brain."

A bead of saliva had accumulated in the corner of his mouth. I eyed it warily. I guessed I was the first person, post-conference, he could download on. I knew that feeling too. I nodded empathically.

"There's so much hope for my patients now, those with destructive behaviors that can damage their lives. We now know that there's hope for, well pretty much, everyone."

He turned to look at me by leaning back into the far corner of his seat, angling his shoulders towards me. His eyes held mine for a moment. As if he knew things about me he shouldn't have known.

I snapped out of my paranoia by looking away. Later, when I replayed the scene in my head, I wondered if I'd smiled a nervous smile, a smile that any psychologist could tell was fake.

The plane tipped its nose towards Florida, giving the shift I needed to end the conversation with the word "interesting" then fumbling through my purse, apparently looking for something, while the psychologist stared blankly ahead. The at-height intimacy was now broken and, by the time the Miami suburbs came into view, he had picked up the in-flight magazine and was flicking through its pages rhythmically.

I felt as if he were aware of my movements, even my thoughts. Shrinks – why are we conditioned to think they can see through us, like some periscope into our minds? I reminded myself that he couldn't, that he was just a guy with a job, on a plane, nothing more.

When the wheels hit the ground, I felt relieved. I could get away from this guy and focus on my next workshop.

*

The last time I'd used the Erin Meyer material on cultural expressions was with a leadership group, all from English-speaking countries. Today, most of the mid-level managers would be from European backgrounds and, according to my briefing sheet from the HR manager, some Russian and Arab backgrounds too. I wondered if I needed some cue cards listing some of the differences in communication so that participants could see, not just hear, the examples.

"In some cultures," I say, "it's common to raise your voice when excited, to touch the person you're speaking to, say, on the arm or shoulder, or to use your hands to accentuate a point." Gentle laughter as I passionately demonstrate.

"In other cultures, such expressions might feel out-of-place or as if it lacks professionalism. Maybe it seems unnecessary to sound excited – for some, we should remain calm and factual at work – or the added emotion is seen as immature." Heads nod in response to my virtual monotone.

"Like almost every aspect of culture, these differences have been studied and measured." I click on the screen, let them soak in the information on the chart.

"As you can see, various cultures are plotted along the continuum of emotional expressiveness or inexpressiveness. Of course, these are all generalizations, but they're based on decades of research, and they involve every culture of our wonderful world."

A guy near the back of the room whispers to a woman sitting next to him, pointing to the screen. Two people turn to chat softly to someone behind them. I let the conversations run.

"So when we look at how most Russians, for example, or Italians or Saudi Arabians communicate, we see that emotion is a common factor in the way they interact. They might use emotive words such as 'We really believe…' or 'I'm passionate about…' or phrases which show intimacy and affection. This is normal. In these cultures, it's the right way to share information."

"But this can make people from other cultures uncomfortable." Pointing to the bottom half of the chart, I say "People from Japan, Germany, even the UK, they tend *not* to include emotive expressions in their dialogue. They speak more factually, objectively. They use fewer bodily and facial expressions."

A guy in a teal-colored shirt looks unconvinced. I watch him. I may be able to use him later.

"But it's when we bring in the confrontation aspect that things get really interesting." I click to add in another continuum on the chart.

"Again, drawing on many different studies across many different sectors, we see there are some cultures that tend to avoid confrontation, and some that are, by and large, comfortable with it."

The man in the teal shirt bobs his head slightly. A little nerve has been hit.

"Take France, for example. Raise your hand if you've visited France or spent some time with someone from there."

"*Longue vie a là France!*" comes a shout from the back of the room.

"*- ou si tu es de là!*" I shout back affectionately. "Or if you are from there!" The room fills with laughter as the dark-headed Frenchman looks proudly around the room. I wait for the raised hands to fall.

"So those of you who have been there, know someone from there, or," I bow respectfully to the Frenchman, "are *from* there, you'll know that an everyday conversation on the street between people from these highly-expressive cultures can sometimes look like they're having an all-out argument, or that there's some sort of problem, right?"

The Meyer material is working. Do I need some visual cues?

"But for those of us from less-expressive, and less confrontational cultures – Denmark, Netherlands, Germany – a discussion about politics in the parking lot is their idea of a very bad day!"

The teal man nods emphatically. It's time to take a gamble. If I've got this right, I can turn to him directly, without offending.

The percussion of laughter and chatter wanes. Then I face teal man and ask, "Do you mind my asking, which culture do you most identify with, sir?"

"Have a guess" he taunts. My instincts confirmed.

"German? Dutch?"

He nods, impressed.

"Would you say that the way in which your culture has been measured in terms of confrontation and emotional expression is accurate?"

"I do."

"Why? Can you please explain?"

He swallows. Then sets it out. "Well ... it has to do with the way that I disagree with people. In Holland, we might say things like 'no that's a stupid idea' or 'I disagree because – .' But here, around all these other people, the Dutch, we've learned to say things like, 'you know, maybe we can do this instead' or things like that. We don't talk like we do back home."

"Very observant, thank you. So, what does that mean when colleagues from places like Mexico or India – places where both emotional expression and a willingness to deal with confrontations – are on the opposite ends of the cultural spectrum?"

Good ol' Erin Meyer. It worked.

*

In my hotel, I laid back into my bed with my fingers linked behind my head. I closed my eyes, imagining physical creases and bulges on my brain, marks of my past, being photographable and in full view of any passing brain scanner.

And what about Dottie's brain? She was only five when her beloved dad left us. What did her brain matter look like? It was interesting how that psychologist talked about the association between grief and executive functions. Good decision-making, mood moderation, delayed gratification, all those traits that parents try to grow in their children to get them safely to adulthood. Dottie certainly seemed to struggle with many of those things.

I sat up and grabbed my laptop, rolling my shoulders as I waited for it to start up. Maybe I could see what other people's pasts looked like, how their experiences of loss recorded themselves in the flesh. Maybe there are new clues as to how to approach Dottie's challenges. And while I was at it, mine too. The conference papers would be a good start.

I scrolled through the events page on the McCormick Place website. The conferences this past week were the True Value Fall Reunion, American Association of Optometry Annual Conference, and Farnsworth Anytime Brands. Nothing about adolescent psychology. He must've got the conference center wrong.

I searched for "adolescent grief conference Chicago" and "pediatric mental health event Chicago." I learned that the LGBTQI+ Health conference was on (why did Google relate it to grief?), who the presenters were in last year's Complex Trauma Institute's conference, and advice from Illinois State Department of Health as to how to set up a trauma-informed youth specialty service.

But I didn't find any reports, or even hints of, a conference on adolescent trauma and psychology held at McCormick

Place. I must've heard him wrong. The conference was probably in Gary, Indiana or maybe Rockford.

One corner of my chest felt heavy, as if a couple of ribs were refusing to flex in unison with their counterparts in the rest of the ribcage.

The menu for the hotel's restaurant lay on the desk near my laptop. I flicked through it, thinking it could be a good night to have a Caesar salad and glass of wine in my room instead of having to face distracting people in the restaurant downstairs. I closed the menu and filled my lungs with air.

At least I'd see Jess this weekend.

Chapter 7

```
CHICAGO - PHOENIX
DEPARTS 8:32 AM
MAY 9, 2022
```

She looked wild with hunger at seeing me. Then again, Jess always looked a little lost and wild.

"Where HAVE you been?!" she exasperated when the Chicago wind pushed me through the door. She was on a bar stool, halfway through a glass of wine. "I thought you were standing me up!"

I gave her a quick peck on the cheek. She smelled like chicken pot pies and, as I pulled away, vanilla scented carpet sprinkles. "Never," I said, straddling the stool next to her. "It was Christopher. He just didn't want me to go. Kept talking about Carl never visiting and I just needed to stay a bit longer, sorry. I should've texted. How are you? Pinot gris please. Haven't seen you in ages."

She smiled her familiar smile. The one that had helped me recover from Tommy Gilbert breaking up with me in 9th grade. The smile that accompanied that first cup of hot tea moments after Dylan was born. "Too busy jet-setting around, aren't you? Not enough time for those of us stuck in Chi-town, huh?" she teased.

"It's not as sexy as it sounds, "I said, sinking my shoulders towards the counter. "Long days in some other company's office – almost always dealing with some sort of conflict. Then back to the hotel for one of the same eight dinners on offer, no matter where you are. Grilled chicken … burritos ... fish of the day. In fact, I've been feeling cut-off, you know, disconnected lately, like the ground beneath my feet is starting to shake."

Jess nodded and, unusually but knowingly, let me go on.

"I know, I've been gone far too much lately, but the work itself is really going well."

"I know my friend. You need to shift down, don't you? But you have something to do that you really believe in. And you're getting so famous now too! An article popped up on my Facebook feed a couple weeks ago – what was it? Modern businesses or something? Anyway, you were quoted and I'm like 'hey everyone, that's my bestie, read this!'"

I had no idea what article she was talking about. Chicago Magazine did something a while back, and a business reporter from the Tribune rang a couple weeks ago but I hadn't seen anything about cultural competency in there yet. I laughed at her animated joy and took a long sip of wine as she went on, Jess-like.

"For me, it's math homework, Brownie camp, laundry – that's all I get to deal with. The other day Kate came home with nits. Remember how much fun those are Cora?" She smiled playfully and crossed her eyes. Her acceptance of her new life with Jack in the suburbs made me want to wrap my arms around her, hoping some of that acceptance would scrape off on me.

"– and Dylan! Isn't he just a gem?! Do you know he messaged me the other day out of the blue? It was so sweet. Something like 'just checking in on my favorite nutty non-relative.'" Jess cackled for a moment, briefly taking in air but then immediately carrying on.

"It reminded me of that time he thanked me for my involvement in his childhood. Remember that? A 'mentor' he called me! I think he was doing some early-twenty-something naval-gazing exercise in his child development class or something. God, I wonder if my little rugrats will ever get to that stage. Anyway, it was great to hear from him and we got to chatting on Messenger about his lovely lady and the job and I thought 'Cora, you did a helluva good job on that one during all those years alone.' Oh my god, did you see the news the other day about the little girl whose parents died in the Ukraine war – or was it Afghanistan? – and her aunt in Maryland wanted to bring her here? There's just so much happening in the world right now and problems we need to fix but – but Dylan, now there's a guy with a purpose. He's going to be one to change the world someday, don't you think? Smart. Driven – like you. He's a special kid but he always has been, hasn't he? Remember that time at Kroger and he was sitting in the cart grinning at everyone? You were pregnant with Dottie and bastard #1 was home drunk as usual. Little Dylan was just flirting with all the old people in between the Rice Krispies and the Fruit Loops – he nearly had a line of seniors following him by the time we got to the checkout!"

I took a fifth sip of wine, easing into the stream of Jess' chatter, enjoying, in my world of talking all day, the pleasantness of only listening.

"So how was New York?" she continued. "Or was it LA? God, you're getting around. What does Christopher think about that?"

I wondered which of those questions she wanted me to answer the most. Probably the last one. "He's okay. I'll just explain that I have work to do. As long as he gets my chocolate chip cookies or brownies, he seems to be doing OK." My heart heavied as I spoke. Was it a lie or just a self-serving stretch of the truth?

"If only *my* men were that easy to please," joked Jess.

"Yes." The wine was getting in. It was so good to be around Jess' wisdom again.

"Jack's been in Vegas for the last few days. Vegas! Sometimes I sit there with our brood of kids and think, what the fuck am I doing here? Whoever gave me the job of looking after these little human beings – not just my own but some other woman's too?! You know –" and here she paused to further whet her busy lips – "who *actually* said I was qualified to do this, other than my own damn ovaries. And that of the other mother's, of course."

"I know what you mean," I interjected quickly before she could go on. "I remember sitting there with the kids, shaping their attitudes, showing them things and thinking: how do I know this stuff? Who said I could do this? Shouldn't there be some larger, more knowledgeable institution raising these creatures?"

Jess looked at me head-on, her blue eyes alive with tannins and adrenaline. "I know! Some processing and development plant for living beings, filled with child development experts that know how to answer questions like "why are you my mommy now?" and "why do you put green stuff in my sandwich?"

We giggled, then ordered another wine. When the young male bartender walked away, Jess said, "Butt dimples in the right place, don't you think?"

"You slut," I teased. "So, what's Jack doing in Vegas?"

"Nice segue." She showed her whitened teeth. "A conference – in between watching pole dancing and slot machines! Just kidding – you know how nerdy he is. I think things are going well at work. Got two more staff, a new contract with some firm in Japan. You know I have nothing to complain about. It's just the hours are so long, the commute. But that's not going to change, is it?"

"Does he travel much?"

"Not really. Most of the time he's home by 6:30 or 7. But that leaves about 60 minutes of mayhem before Kelly goes to bed, then Kate. So there's not a lot of time with Dad. Thank goodness my boys are beyond the bedtime story stage."

I nodded then looked around at the other customers in the bar – a trendy couple who looked like they would make Nordic-looking children together, a group of twentysomethings whose round of tequila shots had just arrived.

I knew it was time to talk to my oldest friend about something that had been niggling at me. I had to be quick. I leapt straight in.

"So, I wanted to talk to you about something. It's a little weird though."

"Yes, please. I need a bit of weird in my boring ol' life. Indulge me!" she cackled naughtily.

"Not that weird Jess!" I waited for her to tune in. "I - I've had the most wonderful and yet peculiar conversations with people on planes lately."

"What sort of people?"

"Just ordinary people. A psychologist, a Chinese American, I don't know, just regular Americans – and a New Zealander. But they seem to be unusually intent on speaking to me about stuff."

"What stuff?"

"I don't know. Their stuff, I guess. But it's starting to seem like – "

"Not surprised. You've always been like that Cora. People have always talked to you for no reason whatsoever. It's like you're wearing a tee-shirt saying, 'Hi my name's Companionable Cora!'"

"Yeah, yeah, yeah" I laughed; I'd heard that one before from Jess. "It's probably just that. But - but sometimes I get the sense that they have something to *tell* me, like they don't just want to make small talk, but something more."

"Maybe they're lonely. Sitting next to someone like you for three and a half hours on a boring plane is probably their dream come true. They probably just spent all day consummating with their devices and, when they're next to a warm live thing like you who's willing to talk," Jess waved her fingers above her head like an aroused peacock, "it's confession time!"

A well-dressed couple on the bar stools next to us cast Jess a quick glance. I pressed the wine glass against my lips and felt sure Jess was right. Maybe I was sounding like a narcissistic crackpot.

It was subject-changing time.

"One guy," I said, leaning towards her further, "was from a town not far from Maroa Bay. Can you believe it? Halfway across the world and we'd both been to that tiny dot of a place. In fact, he admitted that Maroa held a special place for him too; he used to party there with his friends when he was younger."

"Is that right? Six degrees of separation, eh? How cool that he knew about your happy place."

"Talking about it gave me the urge to be there. It's been so long. I really should try to take the kids and Christopher there again soon." I sighed under the weight of that statement. Dylan's college loan, my work schedule, there's no way that was going to happen anytime soon.

"They'd love it," Jess said emphatically.

"They would. And Christopher would be so excited. But it'd be a pain too." I chuckled wryly, remembering how he had, with great fanfare, vomited after Air New Zealand gave him Sprite instead of old-fashioned lemonade. I'd forgotten to remind him of the different terms for his least-favorite, nausea-inducing drink.

"Yes. He would. Dear boy." Jess snickered then raised her eyebrows twice as the bartender walked by again. "You're such a gem, Cora, looking after him all these years. All those decisions about his care you have to make for him, and the staff at Raspberry Hill,"

"– Blueberry"

"– keeping them in line all the time. I saw a kid at the girls' school the other day that totally looked like Christopher at that age. He looked horrified to be around all those other kids, and his mom just stood there like a paralyzed goat rather than giving him a hug or a quiet word. I don't know how you do it with everything else going on. But you do. You've always been there for him."

"He's pretty stable at the moment. The new night supervisor is doing a good job. He really likes her and the other day I caught them playing Payday before bed. It was cute. I walked in and he shouted, "Cora, I'm a millionaire like Carl!"

Jess laughed then said, perhaps too loudly, "Like Carl? Doesn't he know Carl's the only banker in town who doesn't know how to handle money?!"

"Guess not!" I blurted. First husband Tom would've called it a screech.

The bartender came closer to the laughter with a flirtatious smile, "Ladies, I'd offer you another drink, but it sounds to me like you're doing *just fine*."

"Just fine!" I polished off the last sip of chenin blanc or whatever the hell I was drinking.

"Let's do it, Cora," said Jess. "One more for the road, as they say?"

"Nah, another big day tomorrow. Off to Phoenix to fix up other people's problems. Usual story."

*

We were probably above Springfield, Illinois by the time I noticed the man sitting next to me. I was listening to Judas Priest as the plane took off, remembering the soft curve of Jess' motherly shoulders when I hugged her goodbye last night. That vanilla scent.

The man's eyes were intent only on the moving screen of his phone. Jess was right; I just emit a vibe or a body language or something that says I'm a safe place for strangers to put their thoughts. I needed to stop being suspicious about other people's motivations. We're all just individuals traveling along the journey of our lives, trying to make our own ways with the tools and opportunities we have. Strangers on a plane don't really care what the person next to them is up to.

From my window I could see the plane approaching a magnificent towering cumulus shaped like a caped, stooping witch with her grey frontside threatening rain, while her head and sweeping backside glared a blinding white. In the crack between the seat and the wall of the plane, I could see a boy in front of me watching her too. What shape did he see in this willowy act of nature? An inkblot test for air travelers.

Down below, broad rivers broke through the plains, drawing in narrower waterways. I tried counting the connection points, the places where a creek merged into a wide stream or where a pond fed the river. Sometimes, the topography was predictable; a creek meandered then merged into a larger one. Others twirled surprisingly in their paths, curving close to a river then yielding to a rise in the land, or maybe a dam.

As we approached the Mississippi River, everything else was instantly dwarfed by its size. Seeing that impressive waterway on such a spectacular day reminded me of crossing it not so long ago with Bryce. We'd been together for just under a year when he asked me to visit his hometown in Iowa with him. I thought the idea was rather cute, a big-city woman visiting a sleepy little historic town in the Bible belt with her younger boyfriend. We crossed into Iowa over the Dubuque bridge, stopping for a BBQ pork sandwich and a beer.

I was surprised that the town of McGregor had a charm that captivated me so quickly. The faces of the 19th century, double-storied buildings conveyed a time of a bustling city center, even though the pace of life was now slow. Bryce and I hooked our pinkies and strolled along Main Street, stopping at every third window to admire the crocheted knick-knacks or the decorated cakes. The picturesque town threw me into a kind of romantic stupor that seemed to last for days.

There was something about being there with him – some importance, his past – that pulled us closer together, lashing us among the deep brown brick of the streets.

After two days and an extraordinary amount of lovemaking, he said, "You know, it's weird being here with you Cora." His unusual introspective mood captured all of my attention.

"I have all these outdated, you know, teenage memories of this place. This town represents like, a stage of my life that I left behind a million years ago. But being here with you and coming back all these years later it feels like," and I remember him licking his lips slightly as if about ready to taste test a new recipe, "it feels like I'm sort of coming home for the first time. Like I'm grounded here. It's only because you're here with me. I've never felt like this before."

I loved him, I knew that. But my love for Bryce was different to the love I'd had for Tom and Simon. They'd both served a biological or theoretical purpose as actual or stand-in fathers. They both functioned, however briefly, in multiple roles for my children and me.

Bryce had never strived nor felt compelled to fill any role other than as my companion and live-in lover; our relationship had nothing to do with anybody else, no kids, no overarching dreams, no ambition other than our day-to-day enjoyment of each other. His love was simpler, more straightforward than the others.

I sat quietly and listened, smiling a little into his eyes.

"And I feel like I don't want it to change, Cora. I want to keep this going on forever, to be, to be – with you."

It was an unusual moment for us. Later, I remember thinking that in a typical day in our lives, I did a lot more talking to Bryce than vice versa. It was nice to listen to his deep voice as he pushed on.

"So, in this place, I want to see if you would think about, well, what do you think about getting married Cora?"

Looking back, I realized it was the way that moment unfolded, the angled lights and the pine-scented candles and the tenderness in his voice. It was the way I'd noticed the trees, earlier that day, leaning inwards towards both of us, enveloping us as we walked along a woodland trail. It was that Dottie had finally moved out to her own apartment and the liberation I'd felt in the weeks after, a freedom I'd not known since before I'd met Tom. My world now seemed full of possibilities, directions unknown, and fresh prospects for love and life that I needed to feel right then. In a quaint little town in Iowa.

"Say yes, Cora," he said. "Just say yes."

Who would've known that McGregor, Iowa, had a wedding officiant available the next day?

Standing there – needing his hands over my hips, his eyes on mine, his voice calming me further – I didn't ask myself whether getting married for a third time was a good idea. The rest of that indulgent day was filled with food and sex and laughing. Bryce had lined up a cousin and his wife to be our witnesses, and, afterwards, we all went to the only fancy restaurant in town, an outdated place with dark wood paneling and cheap chandeliers called, unpretentiously, Bob's.

When we arrived back to my townhouse in Chicago, life returned to its typical rhythm. Nothing changed much – Bryce went to work at the gym, I took the El to the city every day,

Dottie struggled on, and Dylan got straight As at Northwestern University. But we both felt closer to one another. Well, I certainly felt more connected to him.

That Christmas, our second together, he got me some very luxurious briefs with suspenders from Pleasurements. Christopher started a short-lived painting course at his community house and Sandra kept worrying about what Carl was up to. I made Mom's Beef Stroganoff recipe or a roast on Sunday nights and hoped that at least one of my kids would come eat it with us. Life just marched on.

Until four months later. One fine, spring Chicago morning. April.

I scanned the floor of the plane around my seat. There, under the seat across the aisle, a handkerchief printed with what looked like an Asian script lay loosely. Were the characters Korean or Japanese? Maybe Hanzi, Chinese? I might be able to rescue it when we disembarked.

The man in the middle seat stirred, bumping my shoulder slightly. Thick clouds now blocked my view of the ground, but I guessed the low hills of Missouri were below them. I looked over at the man's screen to see the last scene of La La Land, where they've finished their alternative version of their lives and nod at each other knowingly. If only I could accept my fate like Mia and Sebastian.

If only I could tap dance like them too.

I rounded my shoulders into the curved backrest, hoping the movement would unweight the tension now in my chest. Two more hours until Phoenix. Plenty of time to beat myself up a bit more.

I popped my earbuds in and cranked up Judas Priest's *You've Got Another Thing Comin'* live from San Antonio Center, the salty riffs washing through me in waves.

Chapter 8

```
NASHVILLE – CHICAGO
DEPARTS 10:25 AM
JUNE 7, 2022
```

Telling the Chief Executive of Joysocks.com that I was booked out till October was bittersweet; my client list was growing and satisfied, but my workload was getting harder to manage. I really needed to have that talk with Steve about getting some support and easing back on the weekly travelling.

Nashville had gifted its residents another three perfect days of weather. Every time I'd hopped out of an air-conditioned office block, the Tennessee breeze tickled my face like fingers of warm air from a fan. The sky was constantly cloudless, the sunlight soft. It inspired me to firm up my biceps and wear sundresses.

Dylan and Janey had gone away with friends over the weekend, so I didn't get to see them. Just before I'd boarded the plane, Dylan had texted me something strange. I pulled my phone out of my purse and scrolled through my texts, finding it again.

Gotta talk. Someone rang. A blast from our past. When you home? Love you.

And that overseas number had rung for the third time. I could see now it was a New Zealand number. I'd better email Marilen to check on things.

After two days of workshops, I was looking forward to giving myself some downtime on the short flight home. I'd downloaded some early Black Sabbath for the landing. I closed my eyes in self-satisfaction and let the warm gel slide away my stress.

"Excuse me," said the young woman sitting next to me. "Can you please tell me something?"

"Sure!" I said, flittering my eyes open. I didn't mean to sound so enthusiastic. Companionable Cora must've been at work.

"Do you know where I can get the Metra from the airport? I need to get up to Northwestern University, like, really fast after we land."

Her ponytail bobbed as she spoke. Her lips were thick and moist as they formed words with a slight Tennessee twang. Model material. Manicured. M...

"You'll need to get to the Transfer Station via the Blue Line. We'll land in Terminal 1. They're lots of signs about how to catch the Blue. Once you get downtown, you catch the Red Line up north to Evanston."

She smiled prettily. "Thanks so much. I wondered if it'd be two stops."

"Are you a student there?" I asked.

"Yeah, it's my first year there." She showed her teeth. Perfect. Braced as a teenager. I hoped she now appreciated how much her parents would've spent on her orthodontist bills; Dylan's straight teeth nearly made us homeless. "I'm studying pre-law," she continued. "A little scary, but I'm excited too."

I nodded. "My son graduated from Northwestern last year. English major."

"My parents didn't want me to take pre-law," she blurted out. "They wanted me to do social work or teaching or something like that because I have a sister with intellectual disabilities and I've done, like, a *lot* of things to help her out. And I still will, you know, but I wanted to do something that was more about, like what I wanted to do and not just keep doing what I'd done for her for a long time. You know what I mean?"

"I know what you mean. You needed to make a decision about your life that wasn't based just on what your parents wanted you to do."

"Yeah!" She sounded surprised at my summary. "And my sister is doing a lot better anyway since they put her in the Easton Institute in St Louis."

"I've heard of that. Sounds pretty nice." More than nice. In my frequent visits to their website, I learned that it had recently been rated the best therapeutic school for people with intellectual disabilities in all of America. Some of their students came from Europe to attend. Unique, wrap-around approaches crafted for each individual client. Music therapy, hypnosis, sports therapy, cognitive behavioral therapy – even massage. Previously dependent clients learned to function independently, entitling them to graduate. Most clients graduated within three years. All of this state-of-the-art training would cost a family a mere $210,000 each year - a dream completely out of reach for most American families.

"It is *really* nice," she said, stretching out the letter 'r' into a soft growl. Dottie does that sometimes too, a scratchy sort of voice that's supposed to sound masculine or something. "She's like, *loving* it so much she doesn't want to come home on the weekends anymore, which is both good and bad I guess – but she's starting to read now and they're teaching her how to play the harp. The *harp* – can you believe it?"

"What sort of disability does she have, if you don't mind my asking?"

"Fragile X, moderate. It's like the most common sort of –"

"Yeah, I know all about it."

"Are you, like, a special ed teacher or something?"

"No, my brother has something similar."

"Oh – wow that's weird! So, yeah, because she's learning so much, she seems a lot better in, you know, like, herself. She laughs a lot more than she used to and I like hanging out with her again. It's like she's kind of all-of-a-sudden grown up."

"I'm really glad to hear that," I said, trying hard not to compare her with Dottie, roughly the same age, with all that focus, that compassion.

"There's one drawback though," she said, shrugging her shoulders. "It's *really* expensive."

"I've heard. That's a shame. I'm sure lots of people could benefit from their program if it were cheaper," I said, as her ponytail bobbed again.

I tried to place her somewhere. Belle Meade or Green Hills, one of the historic Nashville suburbs in a renovated manor, or West Meade, with its excellent private schools and scissored lawns.

I imagine one of those manors, erect and proud with four ionic columns flanking the entrance, mirroring the power of the real plantations just a few miles away. Inside, a spacious foyer greets us, with a soaring ceiling centered by a flickering chandelier. A wrought-iron staircase curves upwards to a landing with polished hardwood and exposed beams.

It would've been the house that Mom dreamed of: ordered, cared for, everything in its well-considered place. She would've relished the way that the cushions were balanced on the Chesterfield sofa, poised and ready for impressive visitors.

She would've explored the vast butler's pantry, with its uniformed shelves lined with pink peppercorns and grains of paradise, its clean lines giving way to bursts of brass trim.

Mom. And her unexpected relationship with her houses.

If my childhood home in the suburbs of Chicago were a mental condition, bipolar syndrome would come to mind. Rooms were at once tidy and chaotic. Long forgotten coffee mugs and scattered paper across the floor, and clothes draped over every piece of furniture. But the shelves – oh, the shelves – would hold perfectly arranged books, spines aligned, behind trinkets that stood up in deliberate symmetry. Boxes labeled with clean, block letters served as bookends, as if the design of the shelf were a carefully curated puzzle. Mom was adamant that our dresser drawers were well-organized, yet she tolerated mold growing in neglected glasses on our bedside tables and clothes that lived longer on our bedroom floors than they did in our closets.

For Christopher, she was exceptionally forgiving. After a particularly intense, frantic cleaning one weekend morning, she sighed to her youngest child and said, "it's ok sweetheart, Cora will do it for you later."

I didn't mind. Christopher's life was my life back then; whenever I did anything for myself, the next question was "does Christopher need my help?" I knew I could help him manage his meals, his messes, his frustrations, and almost everything else.

But I couldn't manage Mom's outbursts.

They came every few weeks, usually when Dad had gone on one of his work or fishing trips. We'd hear her cries from the breakfast table and know that it was one of *those* days, when the messes and the disorder just got on top of everything else that was good and well-placed in our lives.

Even though Carl was her oldest, she usually started with me. "Cooooora!" she'd call, as my cereal spoon dropped and my neck stiffened. "Get in here right now! This in NOT ok for a (whatever my age was) -year-old girl like you!"

I'd hear one drawer, then the next, slide violently out of the chest. By the time I got to my bedroom, piles of shirts and pants and possessions would be strewn across the floor, begging to be re-arranged.

"Why do you think this is OK?!" She'd asked, towering over me with an unusual intimidation. "How could you possibly find anything in this mess?!"

I'd sit next to the pile and start folding, nodding my head in agreement. How *was* I supposed to find anything if the white tees weren't next to the blue tees, and those, next to the dark tees? It was a good question.

Carl's efforts at tidiness were short-lived and usually ended in his slamming the door after Mom stomped from his room. It was then that I'd follow her to Christopher, who would be crouching at the end of his bed with his hands protecting his head. Once, in a particularly loud flare-up, he even tried to hide in his closet, but there was so much stuff shoved in it that both his legs were forced to stick out.

Except for the regular rhythm of those tantrums, we were a fairly happy family. In the mornings, Carl and I argued over Rice Bubbles and kitchen space, then we packed our schoolbags as if the fight had never happened. We filled our lives with after-school visits from friends and hot dog days at school lunches. I played softball. Carl played football. Every month or so, we'd head out to Chi-Chi's Mexican or Red Robin for a family meal, with Christopher and I teaming up against Carl for coloring-in competitions on the kids' menu placemats. Mom's outbursts were only minor characters in the shared drama of our childhood.

The well-presented young woman sitting next to me would've no doubt had her own challenges in her suburban upbringing. We all do. I guess.

But maybe her family needn't be as concerned about the Easton Institute's fees as mine had to.

I breathed in, then out, kneading a button on my jacket between my fingers. "You know," I said with as much motherly kindness as I could gather, "I have tons of work to do before we land, so I'm going to get started. Remember, take the Blue Line to the city, then the Red Line up to Evanston."

She nodded, pressing her pink lips together. I switched on my laptop and pretended to do some work before I thought:

what am I trying to prove to this young woman next to me? Can't I just look out the window without feeling guilty?

I watched the color of the winter wheat change subtly as we headed northwards over Kentucky and Indiana. The fields of honey-gold began to show touches of green, evidence of my return to a colder climate. It must've nearly been harvesting time.

Curiosity took me back to the family of the woman next to me. If they could afford to send their other daughter to the most exclusive institute for intellectual disabilities in the country, then surely, they could afford to get the Northwestern student an Uber for her commute from the airport to college.

Families can be funny. Family finances even funnier.

Chapter 9

```
PHOENIX - CHICAGO
DEPARTS 7:30 AM
JUNE 17, 2022
```

After Bryce disappeared, I switched off my emotions. Every day, I'd get up, get dressed and take the El to work. I worked hard. I'd just started at Anderson Bargh, pitching myself to Steve as being able to fill a gap in the cultural competency area of business consultancy. There was a lot to prove. Each night, I came home, made dinner, tried to contact Dottie, reviewed my day's work, planned the next, and went to bed. Feeling my skin against the sheets was as close as I came to feeling sensual.

I filled the chest where Bryce's belongings had been with better things; when that filled up, I bought another and filled that up too. The empty spaces he'd so quickly made in my life were replaced by treasures I could touch. That brought me joy. A different kind of joy.

I kept going. Work, Dottie, Christopher, groceries, Dylan, work, and the occasional visit to the suburbs to see Jess or Sandra. On Sunday mornings, I walked along the lakefront alone and tried to fix a few problems in my head: how to keep Christopher busy; what Dottie should do next; how I could get the larger companies on my client list. As summer approached, the number of Lycra-clad runners on the Chicago lakefront increased. Since Bryce had left, I had no motivation to join them. Walking and thinking were quite enough.

One day, I looked at the calendar above my desk and let myself count. Four months, 13 days since he'd left.

Sometimes, I'd look out the window of the El as it rattled along the Red Line, musing about couples as they moved through the world together. A comfortable sharing of the same space as they lurched along Diversey Avenue, a parallel existence, two figures bound by unseeable strings. I marveled at their ease. How could they know all those faults about each other and yet be so connected? Or I felt spite at their ability to pair. Hadn't their lives yet revealed to them the fact that one individual couldn't live as a part of two?

It's true the world is designed for couples with its double seats in the bus and queen-sized beds. After Bryce, I felt an awkwardness – or was it shame? – of being alone in my mid-forties, as if the aftersmell of rejection wafted from me as I passed.

A larger woman sat down next to me in 26B. I tried to ignore her, but I could feel her fumbling around as she tried to make her frame fit harmoniously with the contour of the seat. It wasn't working. She shoved her elbow into my space. Didn't she know the unwritten rule about keeping to your side of the line directly above the middle of the armrest?

Another tarmac. More little vehicles delivering food, luggage and sewage to different places. Another company to fix. Tiredness, the deep kind, like an undertow that kept pulling me away from where I needed to go. Why couldn't I be popular with businesses in Chicago instead of Phoenix?

I needed to get started on work on this flight. If I didn't do it now, I'd have to do it before Monday, and it'd be great if I could take the whole weekend off. Plus, I needed a distraction from thinking about my conversation with Dylan last night.

I looked out at the runway, expecting for a moment to see Bryce standing there, boyish, bulked-up, bronzed. Instead, I saw rigid painted lines and the Arizona summer sun bouncing off the glaring white concrete, like a mirror.

Straightening my leg, I felt the muscles in my thigh. They didn't feel like they used to. Back then, they were toned and defined. Now, they felt like a pancake, spongey with maple syrup. My back, too, had been giving me problems lately. I leaned forward to arch my lumbar, accidentally brushing my arm against the arm of the woman next to me.

For a second, there was a soft exchange of heat between the skin of our forearms. The spot where her arm touched mine now seemed to surge with blood, a kind of interplay of warmth, a brief but noticeable coming together.

I had to think about Dylan's words. Just once. Just once, then I wouldn't let myself hear the words again.

"Who's been in touch with you? What's this blast from the past?" I'd asked.

"Have a guess."

"Let's see, that cheerleader you dated as a junior – Tammy wasn't it?"

"God mom - no!"

"Cousin Clara?" I asked.

"Nope, but you're closer!"

"Family? Older? No idea Dylan, just let it out."

"Dad!" The word came through my cell phone like an eruption. I blinked as the hot lava hit my ear. The word "Dad" was nearly foreign to me. That word coming out of my son's mouth since forever... did he mean Simon? Surely our two years together didn't render him "Dad" to my firstborn. I said nothing.

"Mom?" said Dylan. "You there?"

"Who?"

"Dad - it was Tom."

He paused. I could only think of the tone of Dylan's voice. Perky. Peppery.

"We talked for about 20 minutes. It was weird ... but he sounded ok. Said he'd been dry for 28 months."

"Is that right?" Parented. That's it.

"Yeah - he wanted to talk to Dottie too, so I gave him her number. Hope that's ok."

"Oh."

"You ok mom?"

"Yeah, I'm ok."

"Anyway, he asked what we were all doing, and I told him, leaving out a few unsavory bits about Dottie."

"Uh-huh."

"He's in South Dakota at the moment, that's all he said. I didn't ask him too many questions, it felt a bit like ... wrong. You know what I mean?"

"Yep."

"But, yeah, it's like – he's the last person in the world I'd expect to hear from, right? He'd called a few times and my phone kept showing an unidentified number, so after three or four calls, I finally picked it up. And there was my long-lost Dad on the other end."

I found myself rubbing my fingers across the edge of the desk in the hotel room. I took a big breath in, holding it for a moment and watching my fingers move back and forth, back and forth. As I exhaled, I realized what I needed to say. Then,

I carefully said it. "How are you feeling about that now Dylan?"

"Like I say, it was a huge surprise, but there was something in his voice that seemed really familiar. He sounded different than I remembered him sounding, but I was so young when he left."

"Seven"

"Yeah, so that's – what – 15 years?"

"You got it."

"He sounded – I don't know – calm. Older I guess."

"How did the conversation end?"

"Nicely. He's going to call again next week. I guess he wants to get to know me – us. That's what it seems like anyway."

"And is that what you want too?"

"Well, I guess so. I mean, I'm telling you about it now and I'm kinda excited about it."

"Ok."

"Mom, I gotta run now. Janey's picking me up in a minute. Just thought you'd like to hear that he called. He called! After all this time. I almost can't believe it. Thought he was dead or something."

Dead. Or something.

"Mom?"

"Yep."

"This must be pretty weird for you too."

I couldn't reply. I could hear him shift slightly.

He waited, then said, "Just wanted to say how much I love you, and that you're such an amazing mother to both of us. And to Uncle Chris."

"Thanks Dylan. Love you too."

I hung up and looked at my phone for a moment. I set it down on the hotel desk, which shined with furniture polish. Two fingertips were now pinker than the others.

The plane engines revved loudly for take-off. The woman in the middle seat pressed forward, unavoidably moving into my space across the center of the armrest. I didn't move away. I waited with my eyes closed for her to shift in her seat again. Hopefully she'll shift towards me.

Neither of us acknowledged each other. As the plane surged forward into our weightless flight, past clumpy stratus, spotty altocumulus, then wispy cirrus clouds, I leaned in closer, towards her warm, caressing skin.

Chapter 10

Maroa Bay
Tuesday, 25 October 2022

My only gripe about Maroa beach is that it falls short of a walk that really gets the heart racing. At just under half a mile, I needed something longer to get my heart rate up for more than twenty minutes.

Grandma had sometimes driven us kids up to the surrounding hills to explore the native woodlands of the peninsula, with their trails winding up through ancient forests peppered with waterfalls and boulders to climb. I packed a light lunch in my backpack and headed north in the rental car.

Since meeting that Māori guy on the plane a few months ago, I wanted to get up to Tita Beach to the waterfall walk Grandma had taken us to – the one we'd talked about on the plane. When I was nine and new to giant waterfalls, it seemed like the biggest, most powerful thing in the world. I'd held my gran's hand tightly as Carl threatened to push me in. The noise, the rush of water, the remoteness of it all; I'd been mesmerized. It would be fun to compare it to my adult reaction now.

I passed through three towns along the main highway north. Growth was everywhere: tidy new neighborhoods with compact, modern houses, new playgrounds and walkways along the beaches, and a widened single-lane bridge that had in the past held up traffic for miles in the busy summer months. I could see why Marilen thought the area needed its own high school. This place was pumping.

At Tita Beach, I parked the car and watched the sea for a while. As a surf beach, the rolling waves were strong and round, but, with the cooler weather and it being a weekday, there were no surfers to watch. The website had said the trail head was at the south end, so I walked along the sand, firm from the outgoing tide.

Stepping onto the trail was like stepping into a different world. Suddenly, it was windless, damp and quiet. The temperature dropped and my shoes slipped on the smooth trail. The crash of waves fell into the barely audible background. Birdsong, all at once, prevailed over everything else.

The irregularities of nature made me uneasy at first. The path was sinuous and knotted with roots, making every step unpredictable. Branches of beech trees reached out across the trail. When I gripped them for stability, their skin felt smooth but buckled, with knobs like bunions on an old woman's foot.

Unlike my movements in corporate hallways and airports with their glossy, uniformed surfaces and perfectly squared tiles, I moved in bursts of unbalanced hobbles. Grandma must've had a tough job getting me and Carl up here all those years ago.

In parts it was friendly and forgiving, then as the hum of the waterfall grew, the steps got steeper and more difficult to negotiate. Sometimes I needed to use my hands to pull my lower body up along the trail.

After half an hour of walking, I stopped, feeling my heart beat loudly and my legs pulse with blood. I cursed my months of too-little physical activity when I should've been going for longer lakefront walks and re-joined a gym. It couldn't be too much further from here.

The beech trees gave way to Coromandel kauri, one of the great native species on this peninsula. Their branches stooped over me like an ancient cloak. Protecting me.

I turned to look behind me in hopes of feeling some small satisfaction at seeing how far I'd come. A flash of unnatural color flickered in the distance. Against the lush greens and patterned bark, a wild blue stood out. A bird? New Zealand had many unusual native birds. Grandma would've taught me their names, but I couldn't remember them now. I squatted to rest and watch.

Through the thick bush I saw the splash of blue again. It was on the trail below me, too big to be a bird. Maybe a group of hikers behind me were catching me up.

The waterfall sounded so close. I filled my lungs with wet air and stood up. A quick burst should get ahead of them – I could enjoy the waterfall alone for a moment. As I rounded a final bend, a mist floated across the trail. I distantly remembered this turn. "We're almost there, Cora. Carl! Wait for Grandma please!"

A massive boulder jutted out of the hill at half the height of the waterfall. It was hugged by thick ferns and kauri trees, opening out to an expansive view of the falls, a perfect viewpoint to observe its powerful grace. Down below, the cauldron was white with ferocious spirals of water spinning in wild circles before falling into a deep pool.

I stood back from the edge of the boulder, empathizing with the fear I'd felt as a child when I was last here. In the face of such force, we feel powerless and humbled, no matter what our age. I wished I had my gran's hand to squeeze this time. I took a step closer, bringing more mist onto my cheeks. My feet felt firm and heavy against the rock.

Then, a new presence behind me. I turned to look, revealing a man in a red bucket hat, faded and loose around his wavy hair. He nodded at me and looked away; a quiet hello and permission to continue my moment alone. I couldn't *not* speak to him. "Hello" I said softly.

"Kia ora," he replied, folding his arms over his blue t-shirt.

Grandma had said 'kia ora' was more than just the way to say hello in New Zealand. "It's wishing you the essence of life, the breath of life – ora."

"Kia ora," I smiled, trying to soften my American 'r'.

He nodded and then looked away again.

I turned to watch the outermost lines of the falls change as different volumes of water roared down the cliff. I watched long-winged birds hover above its drop, using the force of wind generated by the falls to gain lift. The ferns and bush nodded in their own rhythms. Like a gathering cloud, every organism in its orbit was affected by the power of the falls.

The man seemed to be examining something in the bush. I felt like I was interrupting his view of the falls, so I took a couple steps back to allow him to see more widely. He turned his body slightly towards the opening to the falls.

His minty aftersmell lingered in the air. Needing to fill the empty space, I said "Incredible, isn't it?" Straight away I wanted to retract my stupid cliché.

"Yeah," he agreed graciously. "A terrific spot, eh?"

The tonal upturn at the end of his sentence was classic Kiwi.

When I used to spend my Christmases or, twice, my summers in Maroa Bay, I'd return home with three things that my American friends could simply not believe. That summer was actually winter in New Zealand – though not the Chicago version of winter with snow, sub-zero temperatures, and a blistering wind – was nearly incomprehensible to Jess and our friend group. That my Kiwi grandparents weren't rich but alternated between two houses, one of which was on the beachfront, seemed to them like something out of a movie. And that Kiwis often made statements that sounded like questions was a trait my friends couldn't wrap their heads around. Why didn't their comments sound affirmative and absolute, like Americans'?

My pre-teen self would try to mimic the New Zealand intonation when I returned home. My American friends had never wanted or been able to visit a country so far away, and could only imagine a place that was English-speaking, modern and "civilized." but nonetheless different to our own. Speech-wise, my Yankee impersonation could never do justice to the melodic, conversational intonation that the man standing in front of me now used.

I looked at him more closely. Brown skin, dark, wide eyes: probably Māori.

"I came here with my gran when I was around nine," I blurted out. "I wanted to see how much I remembered from back then."

"And did ya?" he asked, taking a step towards me. "Remember much?"

"Yeah. I remember the fear. The fear of falling." I smiled, then suddenly felt fine.

He paused, patiently, before he spoke. "My rellies used to bring me here too," he said. His voice was casual and low, the ends of his words clipped, the vowels swallowed at the back of his throat. "We used to play here as kids, so I like to wander up every once in a while, eh?"

"Nice. So – are you from the area?"

"Yep. Just down around Tairua. You know, down 'round there."

"Oh yeah, I just drove through there from Maroa Bay. I noticed that single lane bridge has finally been widened."

"Too right. 'Bout time too, eh?" He laughed a little, showing a stretch of strong front teeth, with one missing near the back.

He'd released his arms from across his chest and I could now see his frame. His waist narrowed despite it supporting a small potbelly which pushed his t-shirt out a little.

I looked back to the falls, following a line of white water as it crashed its way down, down to the still water.

I said "I'm keen on getting down to that pool down below. Do you know if there's any way to get there?"

"Just, uh, head back down the path here and you'll see a little ridge on the right that heads off - wait. I'll show ya. Follow me."

I protested for a moment, but he marched down the path. Walking below me, his muscles pulsed in his shoulders and neck.

He stopped at a grey-white boulder which dropped sharply to the falls. "Here" he said, pointing to a narrow trail to its side. "It's steep, but it's worth it."

Then, he stuck his foot on the path and carried on. I followed, insisting he needn't bother and that I could make my own way from here, thanks.

"All good," he said. Nodding his chin slightly with a quick smile, then turning back towards the steep trail.

As we approached the pool, my feet slipped on the damp dirt and, squealing lightly, I slid forward to bump his back with my hip. He turned and stopped me sliding with his palm, pressing firmly on my hip.

That brief moment of exchange, like stroking an object from your past, stretching time out like a string pulled outwards at both ends, impregnating the moment with meaning.

"Sorry," I called. "So sorry," trying to regain my balance as quickly as I had lost it.

He chuckled as he pushed against me lightly. Then, as I spun around to face him, he asked, "What's your name? Mine's Tama."

"Cora," I said confidently. "My name's Cora."

"Tēnā koe Cora," he said. It felt like more than a greeting, but I couldn't remember what it meant.

The deep pool stood in juxtaposition to the cauldron above us. Fed by about ten cascades of water around its periphery, the surface was calm and only gently swirling.

"Cold as," he nodded at it, "but you'll feel like a new wahine when you're done."

"What? Get in? I just wanted to look. No way – it's probably colder than the sea and I nearly froze swimming at Maroa yesterday."

He chuckled again from his belly, then whipped off his t-shirt and kicked off his sandals. When I saw him start to unbutton his shorts, I turned away and inspected a kauri branch drooping over the pool. I heard a loud splash and a high "woo-hoo," then spun round to see him treading water somewhat frantically, his smile wide with excitement.

"Come on!" he shouted. "It's beautiful, eh!"

There are people in life who are comfortable with wanting to be comfortable. They move through the world in a constant attempt to avoid pain, however temporary, of any sort. Spawned from the DNA of the hedonists, these people are not risk-takers, seek pleasure more than adventure, and enjoy only a narrow range of climates where arctic cold and desert heat are to be painstakingly avoided.

I'm not one of these people. It seemed like a perfect time to ignore the smirking cold of the water. I was on vacation.

I stripped down to my undies and bra. Tama faced away from me, paddling smoothly. I yelled a proper squeal when my mouth finally emerged from the icy grip of water.

We panted excitedly for a moment, making circles around each other as the exhilaration of cold set in. After a couple of minutes, we both relaxed and floated on our backs, stroking the water lightly.

Tama looked different now. With his hat off and hair pressed back, he seemed slightly changed, more at ease than when he was standing with his arms folded in the damp air above.

"My people, you know my people are from here. They came a thousand years ago. And these rocks," he nodded at the impressive boulders skirting the pool, "they're my ancestors."

My next three words surprised me. "Tell me more."

Tama's chest filled with air. He looked up into the forest and, in a new voice, said "We're from the great Marutūāhu tribes, of the Hauraki, the northwest winds. Our people went to battle with other tribes at first, but then two sisters were married to the sons of the chiefs of the warring tribes. So, we came to live here in peace. We caught eels and foraged food in the kauri groves and built pas – where we could grow our food – in the swamps and on the beaches."

I nodded. Twice – in case he didn't notice my first one.

"My people, they were blessed with food and mokopuna, so many grandchildren to carry on the traditions and our way of life. But then, as the settlers came, some of them turned against each other and wanted to live as the white men did, with muskets, and drink, and so many women. My people gave in to it too. There were lots of mistakes made."

I had reached the end of my ability to tread water. Its temperature had softened into a tolerable coolness. I leaned my arms against a boulder stroked by the sun. Tama paddled next to me and hugged it too.

"The people lost their way and many moved to the city to find work. The pā and the marae couldn't be kept up by the old people who were left behind. People started having to buy food at the shops instead of growing or collecting it themselves. There was never enough money for the oldies to eat well, eh. They started getting sick."

Tama's eyes darted from branch to leaf as he spoke, as if finding the words in the detail of the forest. He didn't look at me. I wondered if he could feel my intense interest.

"Then, when my dad was a young guy, my people said we must go back to the way we lived before. Our people lived in poverty in Auckland, in Wellington, working when they could on the docks. The factories. Or not working at all and living off the dole, government money. Drinking, smoking, fighting and shit. But Mum – she wasn't from here. So when my dad moved her here, she freaked out, eh. She couldn't live that life and ended up moving back to Auckland. Dad and me – we stayed, and we've worked on the marae and the land ever since."

"So, you and your dad moved to the marae." I said slowly. I took a breath, then asked, "What happened to your mum?"

"Stayed there, in Auckland. Got re-married. Had another family. I didn't really see her for a long time, but I had all my aunties and nan here, so I didn't think about her much. My dad and me – we just kinda kept living life."

The questioning inflection at this end of his sentence made me say, "Yeah."

"So here I am, still living life. My cuzzies – some've come back to help out, some just stay for a little while – but me and Dad, we keep trying to make things work and keep planting, keep looking after things."

He turned his head to me now, caught my eyes and blinked a slow blink. Years before, I'd heard an animal psychologist on the radio talking about the behaviors of cats. She'd said that the sleepy, sluggish squint of a cat when looking at a human was a sign of friendship, of warmth, as if to say, "You're my friend and I feel safe with you." I couldn't help but wonder if that's what Tama was saying to me now.

"So – that's what you do? You take care of the marae?"

"Yeah. Lucky, eh? And I look after the lawns for some of the rich people around here. The baches and the little motels and stuff. All these places, they used to be looked after by my people – we didn't own it or nothing, not like that. We just cared for the land, and it gave us what we needed to live. So that's what we've kept trying to do. Only now we use lawn mowers!" he laughed.

My lips were starting to shiver even though the sun had made a quick appearance in the sky. I wanted – suddenly feeling more like a hedonist than before – to feel dry cloth against my skin. Tama swam to the other side of the pool as I lifted myself up to the warm rocks. I lay face down, hugging the warmth of the boulder and letting the dapple of sun dry my back.

Tama fluted his lips, whistled, then listened carefully. In the distance, a similar tune floated back through the forest to us.

"What is it?" I whispered loudly, trying not to disturb the conversation between man and bird.

"Tūī," he grinned. "The singers of the forest."

I watched him, his face cast towards the deep bush. Then, he pulled himself up onto the boulder he was holding onto, his biceps and shoulders hardening, the ends of his dark hair starting to curl as it dried. I could now see a large tattoo encircling his right shoulder. Inked spirals and fronds, mirroring the ferns that surrounded us.

"Wow," was all I could think of to say.

He continued listening carefully, raising his eyebrows then turning his head slightly, eyes leaping from tree to tree.

I closed my eyes. The noise of the falls had drowned out so many sounds, but now, when I focused, I could hear. The chirp of insects, shrill and rhythmic. An orchestra of birds playing different instruments and melodies. Above me, the touch of branches as they brushed each other in the soft wind. Was that low roar in the distance the crash of waves on the beach down below? And my own breath: slow, full, charged. A warm tingle moved across my midriff. It was time I headed back.

I pulled my shirt over my head, feeling instantly smothered by warmth. My jeans and socks stuck to my still-damp skin. When I'd dressed, Tama turned around to face me from the other side of the pool.

I clasped my hands together. "It was so nice meeting you Tama. Thank you for the wonderful stories of your people and for the terrific swim. You're right, it was worth it."

"Do you feel like a different wahine?" he called.

"Wahine?"

"Woman – a different woman."

There was something in his voice that gave the word a richer meaning. Wahine. Woman. Was it a straight translation or, like in every language, did the word mean something more? Grandma would've known.

"Absolutely," I said. "I feel so much better now."

"Catchya later then," he called as I waved and headed back down the trail.

When I left the protection of the forest at the bottom of the trail, the surf waves crashed loudly and the wind hit my cheeks like a slap. I walked back along the beach to the parking lot; a soft rain began to fall. I looked up, letting the droplets move across my face. I felt strong, the force of nature meeting the force of me.

Wahine. Wa-hee-neh. A different woman.

*

As the hot fingers of water massaged my scalp, I moved my head closer to the spout. My skin felt taut and smooth, my inner thighs less wobbly. I moved the towel slowly over my arm and legs, noticing their natural curves and soft indentations.

It'd been a week since I'd spoken to the kids. Dottie didn't pick up my Facetime call, but Dylan did.

With my hair still shrouded in a towel, I turned my camera out the kitchen window to the sea. "Look at that Dylan! Make you wanna come with –"

"Oh my god yes. When do you think that'll be?" This was code from a 22-year-old for "when can you pay for my flights?"

"Maybe we can go halves on the flights next time, now that you're working." Like my boss Steve's contagious southern drawl, my Midwestern accent sounded as if a few Kiwi vowels had now snuck into my speech. "What about Janey, think she'd want to come too?"

"She's sick of me talking about Maroa Bay. She'd *love* it."

"So, how're you all doing there?"

"What? You've frozen on the screen."

I clicked my camera off and rested the phone on the kitchen table. Now I could watch the sea as I talked. "That better?"

"Yep. So, I haven't really talked to Dottie since you left, but we've messaged each other a couple of times and she sounds OK. And you asked me to see Uncle Chris, so I went yesterday – he says he's gotta talk to you and that's it's super important."

"I'll try to get in touch, but he almost never answers his phone. Did he say what it was about?"

"Nope. Just looked me straight in my eyes when he said it. That was kinda weird, he almost never does that."

"Did he otherwise seem OK?"

"Yeah, yeah, I got him a strawberry cheesecake from The Cheesecake Factory and you should've seen his face! He was like: that's amazing!"

"Well done, Dylan. He's always loves seeing you kids."

"I know, I know – I gotta get out there and see him some more."

"Yes please," I teased. He already knew how much that meant to me.

"So how was the conference anyway? Did you nail it Mom?"

"Hmmm, 'nailing it' is not how I would describe my presentation. But it's done and I didn't embarrass the shit out of myself, or my firm."

"Ha! So, what're you going to do today?"

My neck stiffened. I knew I should say what was expected of me: reading, swimming, walking. But I also knew what I'd really be doing.

"Just relaxing," I lied.

"Sounds dreamy. How's Grandpa's house?"

I decided not to remind him that this place was in fact built by his great-grandfather. As they say, most of us can only really relate to the next two, not three, generations up.

"A bit worn down, needs some attention, some repairs actually. It's starting to look like it's seen a lot of years."

I'd been watching an ominous nimbus cloud shifting slowly across the horizon like a grey tank, dark lines of rain slanting beneath it. Its upper holds of precipitation must've held tons and tons of water. I wondered how many tons were emptying into the distant sea.

Dylan went quiet, an unusual moment for my chatty boy. Something hung in that space, something sensitive. What did he want me to ask him? What had been on his mind?

And then I remembered that Tom had been calling and texting both the kids throughout the summer. After decades of their dad's complete neglect of our family, I'd moved from being resentful of his recent efforts to becoming more ambivalent. Just a few weeks ago, Dottie mumbled how her dad had shared with her a recollection of her fourth birthday party and her cake decorated like a soccer ball, the sport she'd just started playing. I'd forgotten that. All I'd remembered from that birthday party was how Tom was so hungover that he couldn't help me get ready for it.

"How's it going with your dad, Dylan?"

"Funny you should ask. He said last week that he's coming to Chicago next month and wants to see us. Wants to meet Janey too. And ... and you too. Would that be ok?"

The grey tank of rain grew larger. Was it heading our way?

"Hmm. I need to think about that Dylan. It was a long time ago. There's, well, there's a lot of stuff I've kept away from you and Dottie all these years."

"I know Mom. We know about his drinking and violence and stuff. We're not burying our heads in the sand about that."

"We? Or you?"

"Dottie too. We talk about it. She's not as distant and stupid as you think she is."

"I do *not* think your sister is stupid Dylan. *Please*." My voice came out harsher than I'd intended.

"I know, I know. It's just that maybe you have this idea that she doesn't have her shit together, but in many ways, she does."

"Does she? What? Can't hold down a job. Relies on me to pay rent sometimes. More interested in drugs than study. What exact 'shit' does she have 'together' Dylan?"

As soon as I'd said it, I was deeply sorry I had. I sounded almost exactly like my mother in one of her outbursts.

He took a breath and let it out slowly. "Mom, I totally understand where you're coming from. Dad – he left you alone with two little kids and he never even tried to make it up to us. You did everything. Now we're just a couple of normal young adults with a lot of stuff to figure out. But now... now we have a chance to have a relationship with the second most important person in our lives. And we want to. Dottie and I want to. The question is – do you?"

Parenting is a million moments of feeling contradictory things all at once. Proud. Worried. Curious about what they may've picked up from you through that strange thing that is osmosis. Concerned about what they may've picked up from you. Frustrated at the things you hadn't done and the things you did. And always, slightly, amazed.

Breathe out Cora, reflect their feelings, acknowledge the harm, gently move on. But the answer to Dylan's question was so complicated.

Rain made little dots on the surface of the sea. There was a day, I now remembered, when Tom and I danced underneath the hard rain at the far end of this beach, the cool raindrops beating hard on my bare shoulders, Tom's arm around my waist. We spun in quick circles as we kissed, wet hair creeping across each other's cheeks, laughing and licking the rain. Every part of our bodies wanting to touch, to exchange something.

"Maybe … maybe I'm ready," I whispered to my son.

Dylan waited. As if he knew, he waited for the fat tear to drop from my chin onto the torn upholstered chair that his great grandfather had found by the side of the road. The chair that his great grandmother had spent hour after hour on, planning my mom's wedding, writing lists of who would sleep where and which neighbors would bring food for all the American guests. The chair on which, one night, when my parents were delayed leaving Auckland and Tom and I arrived alone, he was – after fish and chips and a Speights beer each – probably conceived.

Then he said "Mom, can you turn on your camera now? Let's see if it's a better connection."

I brushed my finger across my face and clicked on the camera. He'd moved his phone closer to his face now, creating, equally, both intimacy and distance. Like talking to the person sitting next to you on a plane.

"That better?"

"Yep," he said. He looked straight at me. I saw Tom's chin, but everything else was mine. "So, if it's ok with you, when Dad comes to Chicago, I'll make a time when we can all get together for dinner. It'll be at a neutral location – pizza or something. Dottie and I will arrive first. Janey will come too – it'll give it a sense of objectivity, nothing serious, you know? Then, a little later, once everyone's nerves have settled down, you can join us. It'll be ok. I promise. If you don't want anything else to do with him after that, that's ok too. OK?"

"OK." The letters floated out slowly, like two furry seeds blown lightly from a Dandelion clock.

"Don't worry. I've got it all covered. And Mom?"

"Hmm?"

"Can you bring me home some Pineapple Lumps? And Minties too please."

"Of course. Love you."

The rain cloud slipped out of view behind the headland. I switched off my phone and listened to two seagulls arguing.

There, that spot on the beach where I'd loved to sit when the kids were young, watching Tom toss them in the air or pull them through the flat waves. It's where I was when, one day, my mom sat down next to me to tell me she had breast cancer, and I pulled into her arms and let her stroke my hair and cry. Where Grandma, when I broke out in some horrible adolescent rash, emerged from the bush at the end of the beach with some heart-shaped leaves, scrunching then pressing them against my skin.

A little cloud, shaped like a cookie, sat alone on the horizon. Where were its tribe, its pairings? Did the rest of them know that, while they sauntered off with different wind currents and ideas of their own, that this little cookie was left there, hovering in solitude, uncomplaining, marching smoothly along as if being alone didn't matter?

    Clouds: I tell you. It does. Your company matters to the singular ones. Come back to the cookie cloud.

Chapter 11

CHICAGO – SAN FRANCISCO
DEPARTS 7.22 AM
JUNE 28, 2022

My hip was very near the face of a guy crunching on peanuts as he stared at his tablet in row 58. So odd, all these strangers next to each other, trying to ignore the lack of space, lining up like dairy cows to be relieved of the liquid inside them. And at 37,000 feet in the air.

I stood three rows back from the toilet with three people in front of me. Almost all the seated passengers facing me had headphones on, but an older couple were napping with neck pillows and eye masks, their mouths agape in tranquility. A round-faced woman snickered at her computer screen, the plane of her shoulders rising with each muffled sound. A young woman looked down at her sleeping infant, gently tucking the blanket around his face. A teenage boy sat next to them, his finger wedged between his teeth as he stared at his phone.

The line was unmoving – someone obviously had some more serious business going on in there. I scanned the group of faces again. They had something deeply in common. A look. An attitude. It was of connection to themselves, as if only they existed in that little moment in this crowded space.

They looked different from the man seated next to me nearer the front of the plane. ` His face, it now seemed, was stretched as if it wasn't really his, as if he was being different on this plane – from his true self on the ground. Compared to these people – slumbering, engaged, relaxed – that guy was ... or wasn't ... what's the word?

Mexican American, he worked with large companies to help them minimize their environmental impact. He'd said that it was nearly impossible to run a company nowadays without working towards reducing its environmental footprint and then reporting against these efforts in the company's bottom line. "If you're looking to do business anywhere, you really need to be dealing with companies who can make a difference to the local environment they operate in." Interesting point.

The toilet door swung open at last and a woman with a slightly apologetic expression pushed past. A waft of shampoo and toothpaste followed her. I moved up a little, trying not to let my hip rub up against the baby's swathed head.

Whatever was ingenuine about the guy seated next to me seemed to be a feature of a lot of people I'd met lately. On planes, now that I thought of it.

I could see their faces in my head: the psychologist, the Chinese woman, the Māori guy from LA. The coincidence of sitting next to someone whose sibling had a similar disability to Christopher's.

My mind was racing by the time it was my turn to use the restroom. Why did the people seated next to me always seem, somehow, different? Or is it just the awkwardness of chatting to someone as you both face forward in plane cabins? Maybe it's because I'm travelling three times more this year than last, that I notice the subtle differences between the nice people I meet on planes and everyone else.

Whatever the reason, I needed to talk to Jess again. Or Sandra, her sensible approach to everything. This time, I wouldn't let them believe that these people were just going about their ordinary business. They needed to know that the topic of our conversations either matched aspects of my own life or were told so purposefully, as if they *should be* relevant to me in some way. I knew it sounded narcissistic, even crazy, imagining that my own life had anything to do with their stories. But that's just it: it *did* seem as if they were trying to tell me something.

When it was my turn to push past the other standing passengers on my way back to my seat, I thought of the word I was looking for.

When it finally came to me, I was shocked – like the moments after childbirth when motherly love slams through your body for the first time, or when you realize at breakfast one day that you no longer love him – by its urgent clarity.

Chapter 12

```
NEW YORK - CHICAGO
DEPARTS 6:40 PM
AUGUST 15, 2022
```

An elegant Asian woman wearing cowboy boots and hat. A Black family with slightly slanted eyes. The flight attendant – Hispanic-looking with an eastern-European accent. Was it Slavic? How did that happen? I would love to hear the story of her.

The ethnic DNA was so well-brewed in the travelers at JFK airport that almost no one appeared to have been spawned from a single ethnic lineage. And if their racial lineage was unmixed, their adoption of other cultures certainly wasn't. It was exciting to take in such diversity.

Although the romance of flying had long ago worn off, I tried to take notice of the little wonders along the way. My yoga teacher would hum *take in the sounds and sights. Accept them all ... don't judge them*. So, I listened to the crackle of a small bag of potato chips opening, to the clink of a lady's bracelets as she moved. I made a tired attempt to appreciate the hug of the seat as I settled in, and to imagine the hundreds of checks, adjustments, re-checks and signoffs that had occurred to get this 150,000-pound machine off the ground today. Despite my efforts, the tedium of travel draped me like a heavy rug.

A man waited patiently in the aisle for a woman to fussily situate her carry-on in the overhead locker. At first, I observed his hands crossing below his waist. Then I looked at his face, and he reminded me suddenly – so suddenly that my heart lurched before I realized it wasn't him – of Simon, with his triangular features and look of slight, constant uncertainty. It was a peculiar look. Distinct. I closed my eyes and saw Simon vividly.

He was sitting at the dining room table, reading the morning paper. His cardigan was thick and pilling, his hair tussled. On any other day I might've thought this was cute, a little sexy, in a Sunday-morning-coffee sort of way.

We'd nearly done it by then, added my two kids to his two kids and made an almost-normal blended family. His kids were great. He said mine were too. With his quiet demeanor, his inquisitive eyes, and his reliability – or was it predictability? – he was everything that Tom could never be.

His wife had died early in life from ovarian cancer, leaving two young boys that were part of the package of making a life with him. I never really figured out if his first marriage was a happy one, but, somehow, I felt like I'd always be a second choice, the next-best option if metastases hadn't robbed him of the better woman.

His grief had had four years to marinate before we met. I couldn't blame his somewhat joyless personality on a sadness that hadn't been dealt with. Our connections were a little prescribed, but occasionally lovely. Our partnership was gratifying in a comfortable way.

That Sunday morning at the kitchen table, Simon had been eating scrambled eggs, along with some bacon that he seemed to be having trouble chewing. He'd looked up at me from his paper, chin twisted in new contortions to deal with, I remember thinking, some unexpectedly tough bits of fat. It was just a flash of this face, a single picture in my mind that had in that instant created a new, overarching narrative for my simmering uncertainties, the loveless moments, the straight, uninteresting path of fate I'd found myself in.

My father's mother had been a proper sort of Chicago native with traditional views about social classes. I remembered when we'd learned that my cousin Clara had become engaged to a handsome plumber, she leaned over to my mother and remarked, in her particular voice that was supposed to sound like a whisper but was intended for all and sundry, "but darling, he's just not our *kind* of people."

On that morning, Grandma Sumberland's words dropped into my head with a crash. It wasn't social class that made Simon different. He was nearly an academic and earned what Grandma Sumberland would've called a "decent living." It was something deeper. The political comments and social observations which had jarred slightly, but which, in my love of the *idea* of marrying someone like him, I had ignored. The little annoyances that I thought might one day swell into unreasonable proportions. The way his boys expressed values that sometimes left my own kids asking, "what did he mean by that?" or "don't they like Black people Mom?"

No, Simon was not my kind of person.

It didn't take long to correct my two-year mistake. After all, I'd done it once before. But unravelling Tom's life from my own had been much, much more complicated.

I told Simon later that month, as his face hung in U-shaped waves and his blue-green irises turned grey. Telling his kids was the hardest; maybe I'd loved them more than their father. Isaac was 12 and already I could imagine him as a young man, teasing some hopeful girl with his intelligent, quirky humor. Scott was only nine and I'd really believed I could save his life by being the mother that his own could not. Maybe, I'd tell myself sometimes, this would be a child that could return my love in the wordless, effortless way that Dottie, back then, and Dylan did, almost every day.

I sometimes wondered if my failure to be the mother that Scott and Isaac yearned for could be made up in some small way, some day.

A week after telling Simon, my kids and I found a little apartment on Lincoln and Addison. Dottie seemed to breeze through the changes in our household, but Dylan's world became, once again, female dominated. He missed the fact-based mumblings of his stepbrothers, their spontaneous wrestling matches, and the way they answered questions in quick, uncomplicated blurts.

Boy 1: This song sucks.

Boy 2: No it doesn't – it's Pink Floyd.

Boy 1: No it isn't, you twat, it's –

Boy 3: Is too, it's Pink Floyd.

Boy 1: How would you know?

Boy 2: It's cool. Listen to the bass.

Boy 3: What bass? It's all guitar.

Boy 2: snort

Boy 1: Dad what's the name of this band?

Simon (looking up from his book): What band?

Boy 1: The one that's doing this song.

Simon: What song?

Boy 2: The one on your UE Boom.

Simon: Who's using my UE Boom?

Boy 1: (Boy 2) is.

Boy 2: Am not. (Boy 3) took it.

Simon: Really? (Boy 3) – did you ask to use my UE Boom?

Boy 3: What?

Simon: Never mind, what's for dinner Cora?

And such went the conversation of our male-oriented household.

A pre-adolescent Dottie and I spoke in different patterns, traversing down alleyways of unstated meanings and emotional side streets that seemed to confound Dylan, especially after we moved out.

Me: Why do you think the girls were, in this case, happy to wear short shorts to Open Day but offended by it at the Student Council dance?

Dottie: That is *so* passive aggressive Mom. What's that about?! I know you don't like Georgie, but you don't have to diss her wardrobe.

Without more testosterone around, it was easier for Dylan to withdraw into his books and fantasy games. Maybe I should've tried harder to cultivate a stronger relationship between Dottie and Dylan back then. Maybe now, he could help Dottie find her way.

Then again, all those books he'd read had made college a breeze for him.

The woman tussling with her carry-on bag finally squared it into the locker. She turned into her row and the Simon-looking man unfolded his hands and eased forward up the aisle.

I leaned my head back onto what American Airlines regarded as a built-in pillow. More like a speed bump.

Where was I going? Shit, there were so many airports. Every bit of tarmac outside the terminals looked pretty much the same. This was my fifth, no, sixth flight this month.

Going home, that's right. RLM Enterprises in Brooklyn. Mexican seasonal workers with Thai owners. Initial assessment: a lot of division and old misunderstandings. Maybe next time, I could start with some activities to find common ground. There was plenty of that: collectivist cultures, commitment to family hierarchies, willingness to conform ...

I wondered if Christopher noticed I hadn't visited this week. Again.

A woman and a pre-school kid took the seats next to me. The child was ushered into the middle seat, then instantly plugged into her tablet before I could even make eye contact. The screen emitted candy floss pinks and blues found nowhere in nature, pulling in the child's eyes like a magnet. No friendly distractions required from me today.

I turned back to the JFK tarmac and wondered how Simon was doing these days. Had the boys turned out alright? Scott would be around 19 by now. God, I wonder what he looks like. Does he still remember me? How much did our two years together affect him, if at all? Maybe Simon had found someone who needed the solid rock of his stability more than me. I hoped so.

In the netted seat pocket, I spotted the rounded end of a plastic bottle poking out from behind the sheet of safety instructions. It was one of those small tubes of blowing bubbles, probably left behind by a parent wanting to entertain their child in less modern ways than the woman sitting next to me.

I pulled the plastic ring out of the bottle and blew gently, hoping the magnetic force of the girl's cartoon would lessen for a moment. Two deliciously playful bubbles danced in the space before me, with one dusting the latch of my tray table. The other bubble moved closer to the child, threatening to do the trick. But the glue held. Her eyes remained fixed on her dancing screen.

I examined the bottle closely, wondering why its designer in some office in Taipei indented the plastic twice around the neck, instead of just once. My fingers instinctively ran across these indentations. That warmth in my chest. I screwed the cap on tightly and slipped it into my purse.

Chapter 13

CHICAGO – NEW YORK
DEPARTS 9:32 AM
AUGUST 22, 2022

Here was the scene inside my head: I started off slower than the audience was expecting, slower than they were used to. My guitar sang through the stadium, the darkness behind me hiding Kirk and Lars. The crowd must've heard this song a hundred times, so I made it sound just different enough to keep them all – every one of those thousands – wondering what I'd do next. I plucked harder and picked up the pace. They screamed. I knew they would. "Nothing Else Matters" never sounded so good.

I looked up to see an attractive Black woman taking the aisle seat in my row, dragging me back to the tarmac at O'Hare airport. I pulled out one earbud but forgot to pause the song.

"Hi," I blinked, thankful she couldn't see inside my head.

Her eyes moved quickly from the dangling earbud pumping out Metallica to my striped business dress and then back up to my face. A forced smile.

I popped the earbud back in and closed my eyes again. This time, the music led me to Carl and Sandra's kitchen on Friday night. Metallica's concert with the San Francisco Symphony played in the background.

Surrounded by her designer tiles and flanked by an enormous stainless-steel stove, Sandra looked like she belonged on a page of a Metropolitan Home magazine. With one hand she stirred risotto lightly, tipping equal measures of Chablis into her wine glass and the pan with the other.

"I don't know, Cora," she said, "I know Carl can be funny about these things. But he seems more private about it lately."

"What do you mean?" I asked, heading closer to the counter to top up my own wine.

"Well, you know how he's always going on about the money, and the bills for Christopher, and wanting to sell this place and get something smaller. But lately, he's not talking about it at all, even though we got a big fat bill from IRS for *four years* of his unpaid taxes while he was self-employed." She rolled her eyes gracefully. I don't know how she does it, but even in moments of frustration she manages to ooze elegance.

"Ouch."

"Ouch is right. As if he hadn't learned from last time. I was livid when I found out." She studied the risotto carefully, letting a thick ringlet of dark hair drop in front of her shoulder. "I know we'll be fine, it won't kill us or anything. We just need to chip away at it, like everything else."

"For sure."

"It's just that Carl is being a little weird and shutting me down when I want to talk about the debts. Says it makes his head hurt. I know what he means!" Sandra tucked the ringlet of hair behind her ear, smiling, but just a little.

"How's the new bank he's with? I would've thought he'd be making the big bucks now. Maybe he's just a little more relaxed about money."

"Maybe. But a lot of his earnings are on commission, so it really depends on his sales figures. That's got to be a bit nerve-wracking each month."

"True," I said, trying to conceal my lack of sisterly sympathy for Carl. Poor Carl. Always demanding Mom and Dad's attention, always the one complaining, the one Dad had to bargain with the principal to keep him in school after screwing up, for the fifth time.

And that night by the bonfire after a high school football game. It sticks with me like a claw in my neck. His crew of friends encircled, jackal-like, around my friends, all younger girls. "Show us your tits!" they shouted, and "Take her down – she wants it!"

Carl laughed louder than them all, then added, "Cora's not worth it – trust me!" to an explosion of menacing laughter.

The next day, when I confronted him about not sticking up for me or my friends, he said "What? You want me to look like a dick cos my lil' sis couldn't handle a little attention?"

One of the great mysteries of my life was how a guy like Carl could attract such an insightful, stunning woman. And then, how he was able to keep her for so long.

Sandra tipped the end of a fork into the risotto, blew softly, and popped it in her mouth. "Let's eat!" she said.

Over dinner, we laughed about Dottie's latest hairdo, talked about one of Sandra's incredibly gifted music students and discussed new anthropological research on the behavior of early human clans. I've always loved spending time with Sandra alone without having to share her with other members of our family.

I looked for a smooth transition into what I really wanted to talk about: my questions about the authenticity of the people sitting next to me on planes.

But there, in her crafted kitchen far away from the background stress of air travel, there didn't seem to be a moment when I could link the admittedly extraordinary idea into the arc of our conversation.

When I finally did mention it, it was clumsy and abrupt. The bottle of Chablis was nearly gone, the dishes rinsed and loaded. As we nestled into her soft leather couch with a cup of peppermint tea, she said my suspicions were understandable, but full of bias.

"Once you have a firmly established idea, you scan the world to confirm that idea, disregarding the other facts that are contrary to it. So, you've met a couple of people who want to tell you about themselves – and we all have a bit of narcissistic tendencies, right? We fish for opportunities to talk about ourselves. And next thing you know, you get this seed of an idea that they're connected in some way, which sets you up to think that the next guy who sits next to you is doing the same thing. Classic confirmation bias. We all do it *all* the time."

"Maybe," I said. "But they're so determined to talk, like there's something else going on. Something bigger."

"You're just easy to talk to and wonderfully chatty," she smiled, gorgeously.

"I don't know – it's like their stories all have something *to do* with me. Like they're linked …" as they fell out of my mouth, my words made my suspicions, hovering now out in the real world, sound like paranoia. "… or something," I finished. Weakly.

Sandra softened her voice and her face. "You know, you've been working so hard and always seem to be shooting off somewhere lately. Maybe you're just getting run down from all the travelling and you're looking for something, I don't know, something more."

I loved my sister-in-law's directness. Its provenance, I'd always thought, came from her being a teacher; she had a professional license, every day, to explain her views, to be listened to, and to impart her opinions and knowledge. I'd made important decisions in my life based on those opinions, delivered by Sandra directly and lovingly.

As I drove home along the lakefront that night, an old emotion returned to my gut, one that I'd felt many times in her years of marriage to my brother. Sandra was closest to Carl's troublemaking; she alone had to deal with the rubble of his misguided actions.

That poor woman.

*

A swirl of soft air swept my face. The woman in the aisle seat rose to her feet. I shifted my purse over with my foot. A slim blonde woman, about my age, made her way into the middle seat.

There she was: my human research subject – if I was bold enough to follow through with it. But how would I do it without sounding like a nutcase? Nevertheless, I had to gather more data, unbiased data, to put a clamp on these stupid suspicions. Once and for all.

The woman moved in quick, direct jerks into the seat next to me. Her motions were curt and precise: one shove of the purse under the seat. Back erect. Click on the seatbelt. Hands folded like a smoothed napkin in her lap. Done.

Sparse puffs of cumulus clouds dotted the sky. I let the Midwest unfold underneath us as I reviewed my plan. Small talk first, then I'd let her lead the conversation. If it turned into another unusual tale, or narrative with a message, then I'd listen and nod. When it was the right moment, I'd stop the conversation, turn, and look at her intentionally. The next few words would be crucial. "Are you really who you say you are?" … sounded too threatening, too weird. I'd try: "That's interesting. So, who asked you to tell me that?" … I knew I'd sound like a screwball if my instincts were completely wrong. "So, did someone put you up to this?" Yes, that would be general enough to be interpreted either way, to see her reaction, to see if I could get her to corroborate my suspicions.

I'd built a career on reading people's expressions and body language. If she was trying to hide her reasons for talking to me, her face would betray her in that first flicker of response. And if it were only my own paranoia speaking, I guess her face would tell me that too.

The plane moved through the clouds like a dancer, sweeping through the gaps of spiraling fronds. I kept my earbuds in – Metallica, mid-80s – as a "don't talk to me" signal until I was ready to engage. We must've been above Pittsburgh when I removed them. I was nervous. I'd never done anything like this before. Companionable Cora wouldn't like this shit.

The woman next to me had been reading a magazine. When I tucked my earbuds in the seat pocket, she rested the magazine on her lap. The door to talk, it seemed, was now open.

"Heading back home?" I began. "Or visiting the Big Apple?"

"Home." Her response was as quick as her movements. "Back home to New York. I was visiting some friends in Chicago."

"That's nice. Where do they live? I'm from Lincoln Park."

"The 'burbs, Clarendon Hills. But we went to the city a couple of times. I just loved it, the Bean, the Art Gallery, the Field Museum. I got worried when the wind picked up from the lake – I don't like wind much. But the sights! What a place."

Her accent was unexpectedly nice to listen to, a mix of subtle southern drawl with the wider, more articulated vowels of the north. Her lips formed the words crisply, giving her linguistic clarity. Maybe there was some distant Eastern European in her ancestral background.

"We do have a wonderful central city. But yours is full of wonders as well. The Guggenheim, The Met. I got to the Whitney Museum last time I was there. Can't get enough of that."

Even as I spoke, I was aware that, if this experiment were to work, I needed to shut up and let her lead the conversation. I ended my testimonials of New York City sites.

Out the window, we were now level with a magnificent cumulus nimbus. It had a circular grey center, like a hurricane, which looked straight into my eyes. For a second, I wondered what the powerful eye might think of the little planes – with miniscule human eyes peering out at it from oval windows – as they crisscrossed around it. Our plane passed it bumpily, revealing a garden of spectacular fluffs of moist cumulostratus behind it. It was jerky up here today.

Several moments passed before she spoke again. If she'd wanted to, it was a polite time to end our brief chat. But she didn't. She kept going. And that was the point.

"So, it sounds like you've spent some time in New York. What for?"

"Work," I said. "Consulting. But I always try to get out at least a couple of hours to feel that incredible thing that is New York."

"Good for you. It's easy to get bogged down in your work. It sounds like you're a specialist in your field. I'm becoming one too and sometimes wonder if that's the right way to go with my career, or whether I should be a generalist with a broader customer base."

I resisted egging her on with words. Instead, I looked at her as blankly as I could.

She continued with her intriguing accent, forming her vowels, it sounded, at the back of her palate. "I specialize in selling historic real estate. I pick up deceased estates and try to make them into something wonderful – to realize the full value for the family."

The woman smiled satisfyingly, as if everyone would agree this is an admirable thing to do.

"One of my clients' great grandfathers had left him a small warehouse on the corner of 82nd and 3rd. Not far from the Met. It was originally a tannery, stunk of old carcasses. Sold to a commercial property investor for $47 million."

"Wow."

Her smile showed her teeth this time. Confirming my bias, she went on. "It's always surprising to me how families don't often realize the financial value of family heirlooms. Maybe it's just an asset of a distant uncle or a little hideaway. Only until it comes to the market after the relative dies do the younger ones realize it's more than an emotional stronghold, but enough money to support them for the rest of their lives. I love bringing that to families."

I didn't respond. The plane lurched forward, causing the child in front of us to say "whoa" loudly.

Her sharp eyes matched her aquiline nose, the shape of her cheekbones snapped into the line of her jaw, and her little ears sat so perfectly on her head that you couldn't imagine they'd belong to anyone else in the world. A jigsaw puzzle where every bit fit cleanly into its place.

My heart felt nearly in my mouth when I first tried to respond. Say it. This is the plan. Say it. But just as my lips parted to speak, I heard her voice again.

"And there was another family that –" I focused on her lips alone, two lipsticked lines that kept pressing together tightly, to form those words which didn't seem like her own. If I was going to say it, I had to say it now.

Now.

"Why are you telling me this?" Maybe my voice trembled. I can't remember.

Her head turned to me suddenly, studying my eyes. The skin under her eyes wrinkled slightly, as if squinting towards my light. The lips stopped moving. Her head leaned forward as if she thought she'd misunderstood me.

Was some mask unveiled, some secret uncovered? Or was it surprise? Was she simply amazed at my boldness and trying to politely conceal that she thought I was bonkers?

Her expression lasted for five seconds. I know this because I held her gaze for two seconds, then started counting to tell my brain to hold on, to track her gaze. "1-2-3." I said inside my head. As my mind formed the number four, something else happened.

I remember the next moments in three parts. First, a sensation of my inner organs pulling upwards to the sky. It was a peculiar thing, but in that moment of feeling a shove in my upper gut, I wondered how organs were attached to my insides: how strong were those fibers, what forces could they bear?

Then, I remember the woman's face. If her expression before was of surprise or exposure, it was now of contortion. Her skin's roundness above her cheekbones formed an unnatural arc, lifting towards her eyes in a single wave. Her eyes wide with fright.

The third sensation was the seatbelt digging sharply into my abdomen. My thighs lifted off the seat. Invisible hands reached underneath my arms and flung them up above my shoulders.

The plane dropped in a sharp diagonal line towards, I thought, Pennsylvania's Amish country.

I don't know what scared me more, the snap of the little trap doors that held the oxygen masks, clicking to release the rubber tubes and plastic yellow cups, or the screams of the people around me, high and primal. My brain moved slowly, taking in each of the sounds with acute awareness, yoga-like, each second spreading out into several more. I thought of Dylan, my handsome boy, and Dottie – what was the last thing I'd said to her?

I grabbed the mask and held it to my face. The air tasted artificial, plastic. My hand shook as I tried to pull the elastic strap over my head. It didn't stay but snapped back in front of my eyes. I took a second breath, ignoring the little strap. There was a voice over the speaker. I didn't understand the words and could only hear my breath. Three ... four.

The plane stabilized quickly. The kid in the seat behind me cried loudly. The adult screamers were now weeping in panicky, muffled cries. A flight attendant, who had been standing when the plane dropped, rose sorely from the floor. The woman's face beside me was still drooping with fear.

"Ladies and gentlemen," said a woman's voice over the speaker, "this is Captain Asberg. We've obviously experienced a sudden loss of altitude. Please remain calm."

The tension in the captain's voice did little to ease my nerves. But her next words did.

"The aircraft is not in danger. The loss of altitude caused a reduction in the air pressure in the main cabin, which triggered the oxygen masks to be released. The air pressure is now close to normal levels, so you can use the masks if you're feeling light-headed or short of breath. Otherwise, you're free to breathe normally. We're moving through significant turbulence so please ensure you remain seated with your seatbelt fastened tightly."

The plane continued to jump around in the sky. If I thought I was feeling vulnerable, I took one look at the woman next to me and was thankful for, comparatively at least, my neurological constitution.

She sat bolt upright, two hands clasped tightly against the cup of her mask. She breathed in frantic, short bursts, her shoulders moving up and down, up and down like a bellow.

I tried to give in to the movement of the plane, letting the mask drop to my lap. Ride the coaster, Cora. Move with the forces. Don't push back.

Someone vomited noisily.

I closed my eyes and thought of Dylan again. I saw him walking down the front stairs of our house in his confident, purposeful style. I held his palm against my cheek and felt calm. I knew I should think of Dottie too. Isn't this what we're supposed to do in these uncertain moments? But the Dottie that brought me calm was young and pure, not the toxic, sullen version of today. The last time I remembered seeing a face that was open to the world, that knew love ... I think she was about 13.

My breathing was regular now. The turbulence still bounced the plane but was easing. The woman next to me had dropped her oxygen mask and let it dangle from the end of her armrest.

We didn't acknowledge each other. We both looked straight ahead. We'd both forgotten, for now, the last thing I'd said to her, a sentence that would've now seemed strange to both of us. Other things mattered. Not some deep suspicion of a nebulous conspiracy about people on planes trying to convince me of something.

Cora, you're ridiculous. Go home and hug your kids. Your brothers.

Interstice

Above Southern Pennsylvania
August 22, 2022

We join in weights that vary Water droplets latent with energy drooped with oxygen ready to travel again or to rest We are pushed up to the skies by heat From every direction we appear like shapes or compact systems But we're much more complex more multitudinous than your sciences know We have unseen layers and behaviors that condense and penetrate and expand Then bind

    Your blunt categories apply to merely a singular moment in time You name us "cumulus" or "cirrus" but soon we will move to other indistinct formations Invisible and shaped by nature's greatest forces Almost everything about us will change Our weight Pressure Locations We connect and disconnect from vast systems governed by variables too many for you to fully understand

Our powers of observation are strong When we drop as fog we peer into your houses and cars to understand you more When we see your planes passing we latch onto them and listen through thick windows Rain drops falling to earth provide the most interesting views of almost every aspect of your lives

Today some of us watched your faces as we clung to the windows of your plane We knew what was coming – the downward force when thermal uplift needs to find equilibrium The towering cumulus rebalanced itself by pushing downwards Taking your plane with it

What is predictable energy to us is unforeseen and frightening to you We heard you scream We saw you clutch for oxygen masks Your breathing changed

We tell ourselves not to revel in another species' terror but there is an undeniable pull in witnessing how other organisms react when faced with the same colossal forces as ourselves

Chapter 14

Maroa Bay
Wednesday, 26 October 2022

Remnants of a dream clung to the corners of my consciousness long after I woke – of warm syrup oozing upwards from my toes to my hair, transforming me from flesh to object. First, the ooze changed my body into crinkly candy wrappers from my childhood, then stones from the beach. Around my hips, my body became wet sand. My shoulders changed to the hills that stood on the periphery of Maroa Bay. Like Tama's ancestors, I was becoming the land and its treasures.

I held this image of myself in my head as I slowly dressed, pulling a T-shirt over the hills of the Bay and leggings over its sand and stones. I ran my hands down my warm abdomen, enjoying my own touch, flesh on flesh, even if it was only my own.

Def Leppard's *Pour Some Sugar on Me* worked well with my coffee. As music and caffeine synergized, I slipped into a buoyant mood. With no one else staying in the house, I wouldn't have to feign the need for a nap or invent some reason for my absence as I lingered in my secret room.

I had no place to be, no family to organize, no meetings to attend, no workshops to deliver. Another long, delicious day to fill as I pleased.

The caps of the waves shimmered, bright and taking shape, like thoughts beginning to surface.

Now, I could see that the work I'd been doing at Anderson Bargh had been growing steadily intense. I can't remember ever having worked so hard and so frequently. Back when the kids were at home, my boundaries around work had been clear: weekday evenings for the kids, weekends for my wider family, and, if I was really organized, there might be time for exercise or seeing friends.

But these past two years – since Bryce left, now that I think of it – those boundaries had slipped with fewer responsibilities at home and Steve's gentle but constant pressure to bill our clients. As friendly as he was, my boss knew how to squeeze a lot of work out of his lucrative consultants.

Maybe there was something more going on too. In the busy days of solo parenting, supporting Christopher, and then, trying to spend time with my new boyfriend-come-husband, I'd felt needed in every part of my life. If my kids weren't drawing on my energy, the rest of my life would be.

In one such week, sometime before I met Bryce, Dottie was caught buying pot outside her school's gate. Dylan learned that he hadn't received a scholarship to college, so his fees next year would be exorbitant. Blueberry Hill rang to say Christopher needed to go to an emergency dentist and Jess was having her wedding shower. That morning, our slow-flushing toilet had finally refused to flush at all.

I sat at work on a Thursday morning with my head in my hands and realized that almost every aspect of my life needed attention. Family, finances, friends, feces. There didn't seem to be enough of me to go around. That day, like so many others in my life, I wondered what things would've been like if Tom and I had stayed together. Imagine sharing the daily and far-reaching duties of life with another human being. What could it have been like to have a real father in my children's lives, instead of two different versions of stepfathers, one self-absorbed uncle who never paid much attention anyway, and another uncle who needed my kids more than they needed him? Why had my life turned out to be one where I always had to soldier on, alone?

Maybe it was the months and years of busyness and pressures before I met Bryce that inspired my decision to date a younger, more carefree man. Instead of helping me manage life's responsibilities, Bryce encouraged me to step away from them. I couldn't help but wonder if I'd been more involved in Dottie's direction-setting during those years, maybe she would now actually have some direction.

With Bryce gone and the kids more independent, a space in my life that I was used to expending on others had opened up.

Maybe my work had snuck in to lay claim to that space. As one set of responsibilities shrunk, another grew.

Huh. The insights that can happen on a beach far away from Chicago with a good song and strong coffee. And my body was winding down. The tension in my neck was easing, my skin was starting to look brighter and clearer. My limbs, strong and nimble. Maroa Bay had always felt good.

What I should do was to start my own business. If Steve refused to take on someone to work alongside me with my clients, I didn't have to keep working for him. I had the skills and contacts to continue my consultancy work without the need for a firm like Anderson Bargh. I sometimes found myself doing the figures in my head: two to three consultancy gigs a month would provide the same income, if I were self-employed, as I earn now. Two to three! I can't remember the last time I delivered so few workshops and reports to my clients. What could I do with all that extra time in my life?

A year's salary, I reckon. That's all it would take for me to set up my own business. No doubt Steve would legally block me from taking my clients with me, but with my reputation and some good referrals, I could rebuild my client base in a few months.

Then there's running costs, accountancy fees, printing – I would have to make all my own travel plans and, what about a web presence? Greg at work was so good keeping my online material fresh. And what would I do without Arlene keeping it real as she gracefully juggled all the office balls?

I rinsed my cup and examined the sky. Cumulonimbus clouds, southbound. Grandma would've said "A northerly wind – warm and wet, little ones!" I wouldn't mind. A late morning back in the darkness of my little room sounded just right.

My phone beeped. Probably Christopher – dang it! I'd forgotten to ring him after Dylan had asked me to. I'm just so slack, he must think I've forgotten all about him. Mom would be rolling over in her grave right now.

I picked up the phone - a text from Marilen. "2pm OK for that chat?"

2pm. Would that give me enough time to explore all the way back to the shadows?

"See you then!" I typed.

*

I must've been about 10 years old when I'd worked out that I could call the cavernous closet my very own. At first, I used it to store my sea treasures and other collectables that I'd picked up in Maroa, or on the journey to New Zealand.

Mom might pop in and say "Dear me, Cora, you sure do have a lot of stuff" or "Haven't you got enough paper wrappers? It's starting to look like a dump in here." She never really tried to understand the effect my treasures had on me.

By the time I started looking and sounding like a raspy teen who wanted to be alone, she and everyone else stopped visiting the tiny room altogether. I was 16 when I lied about losing the key to its door; from then on, the family seemed to forget about the dark space entirely.

Sometimes Grandma would call from the kitchen, saying "The tide's up now Cora, let's go for a swim" or "Time for afternoon tea, darling." but I could usually escape these demands by acting tired or as if I'd eaten too much for lunch. Besides, Carl kept the adults busy enough with his efforts to fish or explore the headlands and Christopher too, with his constant need for activity. Maybe it was convenient for them to leave me alone.

The old air weighs heavy with dust. I try to walk past the first narrow passageway, stopping only to touch a dented can that I'd drunk my first beer out of. Jess and I had shared it, though it tasted gross, then got into a burping contest outside Dan Parker's party.

Stepping forward, treasures fall to the floor from the brush of my shoulders. I reach out to try to touch them all – the travel-sized empty bottles, a set of tiny plant pots, stuffed toy animals – but they join the others carpeting the wooden floor as I step forward again.

There are many extraordinary things about my room, including its L-shape. Before access had been blocked off, it had been a wide closet for the adjacent bedroom with a narrow storage area running at the back of it, along the house's eaves. When the door had been moved into the backroom, it created two interconnected hallways joined by a 90-degree corner.

I turn into the second chamber. My heart slows and my breathing deepens. The smell becomes lustier and still.

The corner of the 'L' blocks the light as I approach the end of the chamber. Here, in the furthermost reaches is a high mound. Well, it had once been a mound and is now more like a floor-to-ceiling sloping wall of treasures. The shadows.

If I needed light, I'd aim a flashlight into the area. But I preferred no light at all. Just me and my most valued treasures.

Years ago, I'd invented a game where I'd reach into the center of the pile, wriggle my hand around, and grasp one of the items. Without withdrawing it, I'd outline its shape in my fingers, trying to figure out which of my possessions it was. With it came the memory of the place, the smells, and emotions of my rescuing it from the world, of bringing it here, to safety, to be loved. Many of my most treasured things were held deep inside the mound, protected by the clutch of other objects.

I wave my hand firmly into the center of the hoard, squeezing my fingers together in search of a prize. There, a shape, distantly remembered. Soft, flat. I pulled it towards me as treasures tumble towards the floor.

I clutched it to my chest. The day that Bryce had finally agreed to come to New Zealand with me. He often agreed with most of my ideas. But not that one.

"Why do we need to leave the US when we have so many amazing places to go right on our back doorstep?" he said, his red, wet lips moving fast. "It costs a fortune and it's just, sorry but, just another beach!"

The hairs on the back of my neck prickled at this idea. Two beers in, I pushed back. "No, it's not the same as Clearwater or – or Santa Monica or something. It's tiny, it's remote and it's a major part of my life. You don't understand what it's like there, Bryce. You just have to visit and see for yourself. You'll see its magic and how it can hold you there in a way that is hard to explain. It's got this, this – I don't know, this power that makes you feel really, really good, and strong."

"Cora, it's my job to feel strong, thank you."

"No not in that way. It's bigger than muscle mass or quad strength. Come on Bryce. Why is it such a problem to just – just visit?"

"Look. I make $19 bucks an hour at the gym. You think I want to spend a year's savings on going to some random place that I've never heard of, on an island in the middle of the Pacific Ocean?"

Even in his anger, I found myself tracing the taut lines of his neck, mapped like rivers that needed to be followed.

"And come on," he continued, "even you have to admit it's all very woo-woo – since when have you been into all this 'bigger than thou' shit?"

"What do mean? Woo-woo?"

"You come home from work and talk about the guys you train. They have all these weird beliefs about spirits, gods, energy – whatever. Seems like you're starting to believe it too. Or you're just too nice or empathetic to really challenge the fact that it's all a load of bullshit and you're not brave enough to say it is."

His words slapped me hard. I reached down towards my bedside table to find something, anything. A miniature figurine of a deer I'd found outside of work one day had antlers that I could run my fingers over.

Bryce had no idea what it was like in the real world. He dealt with all his white, upper-middle-class clients who presented to him holding protein shakes and wearing carefully-curated active wear, convinced that the world worked one way and one way only. He had never really experienced how many migrant Americans brought with them entire systems of belief – great religions, paganism, spiritual worldviews, ways of understanding the universe that had existed long before his tidy, hour-long personal training sessions did.

I breathed, two, three. Calmed my vocal chords before saying in an almost-whisper. "And what does that have to do with you coming to Maroa Bay?"

Bryce touched his hair. Cute. Then said "Like – you're making me feel bad or something 'cause I don't feel this huge, mystical draw that you have to that place. Like I should listen to some higher fucking powers or something."

And then, as an afterthought, he almost yelled. "And yet you know I'm not religious like that!"

I blinked. "I didn't mean to do that. I didn't mean to give you the impression that I cared about that stuff."

My dad had had a typical American Christian worldview – Christmas, the Ten Commandments, prayers before Thanksgiving dinner. A broad, easy faith that didn't demand too much.

But Mom had brought something else entirely into our family's ecosystem of spiritual ideas.

Brona had taught us to regard nature as if it were alive. As if it had a character and a plan. Mother Nature was careful and wise, she'd explained, and always knew more than us. Plants that grew in unexpected, wiry patterns were guided, she'd said, by an invisible map. Seasons brought changes in our habits and behaviours – sleep times, meals, exercise levels – that were non-negotiable. Where there was a decision to be made, we would first consider the evolutionary and natural reasons before they could be usurped by more cognitive ones.

The certainty of my mother's partnership with forces larger than herself may've stayed with me, but I'd never thought they'd barreled through into my own life, as they had hers.

"But you DO care about that stuff," Bryce said. "Whether you realize it or not. You seem to think there's power or, Christ, even some sort of magic in the world around you."

Under his breath, he added, stabbing me more, "Fucking weird." I stroked the head of the deer harder.

I knew that some things were better left ignored. I pulled back to my corporate manner. Confident. Concise. Clear. Come on Cora, you can fix this.

"Bryce, I understand your thinking – it *is* a long way to go. Look, I can pay for your flights, and while you're there, it's all provided for, so you just need to find the time off work to make it happen.

His arm rose to the top of the doorframe, new curves forming around his triceps and forearms.

"I really, really want you to come and see that little part of who I am and what has made me. Maroa Bay is a big part of that. I need you there to experience it with me."

He took a step towards me, the sign I needed. I matched his show. When we met, he stroked my hair and moved his other hand across my waist. That familiar line of energy had formed between our eyes. I moved my hands to his hips and pulled them slightly towards mine. "Please Bryce," I whispered, "this is important to me. Please come."

He kissed me, sweeping my hair back from my face with two hands and then, taking two fistfuls and tugging back, forcing my chin up. The move served as a sort of switch; we clicked into a frenzy. I could smell the soft scent of a day's worth of gym sweat filled with pheromones, like wet rosemary or the tinge of garlic.

As I remembered this scene, I watched our bodies from a third person perspective, as if it wasn't me, but some other woman pressed against the wall by Bryce's frame. I watched his forearms flex as he squeezed my shoulders, then brushed my neck. I saw his hips moving rhythmically, then mine, in powerful waves.

With him, the pathways to sex were never the same. There were no patterns of foreplay, no hints of what might come next. It reminded me to some degree of sex with Tom all those years ago – kitchen chairs, storerooms of bars, youthful, uncaring sex – but now, by the time Bryce got to me, I knew so much more about my body and the things it could do. And I'd been getting stronger at the gym. Jess had said I was getting "toyboy abs." If there were themes in mine and Bryce's sex life, pasta seemed to reappear. And rain. Running in it, then de-robing.

After that argument, and to remember the intensity of our lovemaking, I rummaged through his gym bag to find something to mark that day. Not his shorts, not his socks, there it was: a small hand towel that he used to wipe off during workouts. He'd think he'd left it in the locker room.

In my secret room on the other side of the world, I pulled the towel over my face, breathing in its soured fumes. Heat surged throughout my body, through my core, radiating through my limbs, down to my toes.

*

We sat facing the sea in lawn chairs dotted with rust. The chair's faded fabric seemed to perk up when Marilen's bright floral shirt pressed against it. I made gin and tonics that sparkled in the afternoon light, the ice cubes rattling against the glass as we sipped.

Despite the scene, Marilen didn't seem relaxed. Our chatter felt more forced than it had been earlier in the week. I sensed she might be in a hurry to get back to her office.

"Things have moved quickly since we spoke on Monday, Cora. I wanted to talk you through what's been happening," she said, the pitch of her voice lowering.

"Moved? What do you mean? Do you mean the creepy phone call you got from Auckland?"

Marilen smiled – perhaps a little stiffly. "Apparently, the developers hoping to build the hotel have not only bought the two sections near the car park, but they've got the Townsends and Craycrofts to a point where they're discussing a price."

Townsends: a multi-generational family who loved crayfishing and scuba diving. Their kids were a bit older than mine – maybe there'd be grandkids by now. Craycrofts: the elderly couple had been AirBnB-ing their place for years. These beach houses on either side of ours mostly stood empty during our visits, but were no doubt filled with people during peak times of the year.

"OK," I said slowly. "So both our neighbors' places might be sold – "

"I think we can say '*will* be sold'. Price isn't a concern for these developers. They can pay whatever it takes."

"Whatever it takes to do what?"

Marilen jingled the shrinking ice cubes in her glass, then knocked back a large mouthful. She cast her eyes to the far end of the beach, then to the headland closest to us. Her bosom moved up and, as she exhaled, said "Build a hotel – an EcoWorld resort, at this end of the beach. They have plans to build on all six sections on this end."

"All six sections? You mean, wipe out all these baches and put a parking lot in? Wait. Isn't there a song about that?" The gin was going to my head. I hummed the tune first and then sang "Pave paradise and put in a parking lot."

Marilen let herself smile a little this time. Then said, without looking at me, "No, the carpark will be where the playground and barbecue area is, over there." She pointed flaccidly.

"A parking lot instead of a barbecue? Are you joking?"

"No, I'm not." She stared out at the sea.

"What about the bach at the end here, two down. Who owns that now?"

"A young family from Auckland. They bought it just before the pandemic and ended up spending lots of time out here during the national lockdowns. For them, it'll just be a matter of price so they can afford to buy another holiday place along the Coromandel."

"So, they're ready to sell too?"

She nodded a reluctant nod.

"So," I turned to face Marilen. Drawing on years of experience as a cultural trainer, I tried to sound curious, not judgmental, when I said "Are you saying you support this move to transform Maroa Bay into a – a resort – an eco-resort?"

Marilen moved in her seat and took a final sip of gin. The ice cubes, in the sunshine of late spring, were no longer audible. "Everywhere around here is changing. The Coromandel Peninsula of my childhood and yours can't be sustained. It's – it's all so full of people now, the beaches aren't isolated anymore and the townships, well, they're just not keeping up with the demands of modern living."

Marilen shifted forward in the chair, put her empty glass in the sand and relaxed her shoulders. "You know, I have a cousin in Tairua who drives to Hamilton – almost two hours away – just to take her kid for medical treatment every couple of weeks. She can't find work as a dental assistant around here, so when they offer it, she drives an hour and a half to Tauranga to fill in for someone for $24 an hour. New Zealand dollars. Bugger all. New Zealand is this tiny little country, and the Coromandel isn't Auckland or Wellington or Christchurch getting all the attention. It's hard to get resources over here, even as the region gets bigger. I think this area is full of opportunities and we need more businesses and more people to improve our roads, build more schools, lift the economy, you know?"

I was surprised to hear Marilen, who'd always seemed loyal to New Zealand's more socialist version of government, talking about growth. The way this economic theory was encroaching on my own little slice of paradise was unsettling. Still, I nodded, encouraging her to continue.

"So, the other day, I meet this family from Thailand who want to move here. To Maroa Bay. They've been living in Auckland for, like, ten years, have three kids, and just want to quit that urban way of life. They're from a farming family in Thailand and were looking at a property up in the hills that was for sale that would be perfect for growing coriander or basil or even commercial flowers. Everything was right – the aspect of the sun, the three-bedroom house, the four acres of fertile land. But you know why they couldn't move here?"

"Why?"

"'Cos the bloody bus doesn't go near the property! The school is 40 kilometers away and they'd have to drive them in and back every day. Bloody price of petrol, and two hours every day, all that. Plus, there's no music lessons, no soccer, no nothing out here for those kids."

"So, you think that by building a hotel on this beach families like that would move here?"

"No, well yes, they'd have more of a bleeding chance to, wouldn't they? I mean, if we could grow this place to a few more thousand every year, we could afford all that stuff. Right now, we're still too small and insignificant to get the politicians to notice us."

"Even with all those new developments and suburbs popping up all over the place?"

"Even with those. Every second new house is a holiday home for an Aucklander. We need people who live here and who *love it* here. People that buy into the area and work here and form communities, year-round. Only *that* will bring the resources to make this peninsula the place it should be."

In all my years of knowing Marilen, I'd never seen her this amped up. This was her reason. Her new purpose.

"But that's the big picture," I said. "A family like ours doesn't have a lot to do with what's going on in New Zealand. We're so far away and just cherish this place for our times here. We may pay property taxes, but we don't have much to do with local politics and all that."

"Really?" Marilen brushed a hand through one side of her hair.

"Yeah," I replied, hesitant about what I'd just said.

"I feel that's just a bit short-sighted, Cora. I mean, you've been coming and going from this place your entire life. You talk about how much it means to you, the memories, the connection to this beach. Doesn't what happens here matter to you?"

It was an interesting question. Maroa Bay's future mattered to me as much as it affected our holidays, visitors, and costs. That much was true. But did I care about the longer-term wellbeing of the area or things that happened here while I was living my life in Chicago? Did its future matter to me in the same way the shoreline of Lake Michigan or the school district of Lincoln Park mattered? Honestly? I needed to think about that.

Marilen couldn't read my thoughts, but she read my face and quickly, in non-confrontational Kiwi-style, pulled back.

"I guess for holidaymakers like you, it's taxes and the tourism market that affect you most. But for residents like me, and the locals and especially Māori around here, these changes make a big difference to us. They last for a long time and affect almost every aspect of our lives. I mean, I remember my dad telling me the story of my granddad supporting all the forestry companies when they wanted to start planting pine trees here in the Coromandel. This was like in the 1940s and there was nothing but land and native forests, a few beach developments, and little Māori settlements out here. A lot of people hated the idea of forestry coming out here, and others thought it was the best way for this region to start being useful and to get jobs and money here.

"Some of Granddad's neighbors were majorly anti-logging. They kept harping on about it and one time, when they were over for a barbie and after a couple of beers, Granddad said, 'Well, what the hell do you think we're going to do for work around here? Scratch our balls?'" Marilen screwed up her face and belly laughed, her light mood starting to return.

"Everyone laughed, then one bloke grabbed a beer and started singing 'For He's a Jolly Good Fellow' at the top of his lungs!"

Marilen shook her head and said "Classic. Anyway, you look at what the pine forests have brought to this area, decades later. We wouldn't have the roads and the employment we do around here without the forestry companies making it all happen.

"We've always argued about how much of the real world we're willing to let in. But people are sick of living as if cellular towers and decent bridges aren't important. They are. It's time we started working with the right companies to bring about the changes we need here."

The tide crawled closer to our bare feet. I watched an extra-large wave zoom across the sand, nearly reaching our toes.

"And EcoWorld is the right company to do that?" I asked.

"Well, they seem good. Been working with environmental groups and they own those new cottages as you come into the village. New motel being built in Tairua too. They're starting small, but this new beach development will be a much bigger project for them. I guess that's why they're so willing to pay so much."

"How much?"

"Don't know exactly. But what I've heard is that the Craycrofts' is going for over a million and a half, and the Townsends', bigger that one, maybe almost two? Your section's roughly the same size."

Two million NZ dollars. For the wobbly house that Grandpa built. I quickly converted that to US dollars, then divided by three for my portion. Enough money to live mortgage-free, get Dylan's college paid off, fix the kitchen, give Dottie a few more options. We could sort something better for Christopher and give him more reason to get up in the mornings.

I burrowed my toes into the sand. It felt cool underneath. I imagined the seal of my secret vault being pierced, exposing its narrow tunnel, then slipping beneath the sand into my private sand cave, lined with a million treasures.

A cold wave rose around our ankles. Marilen swore and cackled loudly at the same time, picking up the old lawn chairs while I chased her plastic glass, floating back to sea.

As we walked back to the house, I looked at the bent garage door and the cracks in the concrete path surrounding the bach.

"Can't believe this old place is worth that much," I said. "OK then, I'll think about what you said. I'll talk to my brothers next week when I get back. Hey – I'm heading up the beach for a walk. Wanna come?"

"No thanks. I'm due back at the office," she said, rolling her eyes playfully.

I walked against a light onshore wind. Breathing new energy into my life could mean a lot for me and the kids. Something to set different things in motion, like that guy said who I'd met on the plane – the psychologist who went to some unnamed conference. Letting go of links to the past: houses, jobs, and even relationships – these fresh starts can be liberating, leading to new beginnings and actual, physiological repair.

A one-off cash injection might do just that. Maybe it was time to let the splendor of Maroa Bay go.

Chapter 15

```
CHICAGO - LOS ANGELES
   DEPARTS 8:55 AM
  SEPTEMBER 5, 2022
```

My American Airlines air points were adding up. At the last minute, I was upgraded to Business Class. The bucket leather seat felt like a warm body was holding me from behind. Spooning me.

From Row 2, I watched the other passengers coming in from the tarmac – for some reason the airbridge wasn't being used, so we'd walked uniformly between the yellow lines, bending into a strong wind. The faces appearing in the calm air of the plane looked slightly squashed, exasperated. Fingers quickly moved to flatten hair and clothing. One woman demanded the flight attendant confirm there were no more steps to climb. A man with rugged features looked somewhat thrilled at the hit of nature he'd just experienced after so many days in the concrete and glass streets of my city. Did the Inuit people use these same expressions when they dipped into their igloos?

I could see right into the cockpit. The switches and buttons still held a wonder for me: what did they all do? How often were they used? Which ones were used in my flight which dropped in altitude?

A forearm intercepted my view of the plane's dashboard. The muscles were well defined, almost bulky, with a thin scattering of darkish hair. I couldn't help but think of that forearm pressing the inside of my own arm against a pillow.

A tablet was passed from the hand attached to this body part. The tendons hardened as they reached across the device. Who was connected to this limb? What did he smell like?

Back to LA. It was tough work. The genesis of many of the cultural clashes at Drumme Manufacturing was, I now realized, a particular manager who had a permanent look of disdain on his face, as if some tartness had been tasted and then frozen in his expression.

Originally from India, he didn't like the Filipino staff. It was as simple as that – he didn't like them, and he didn't understand them. He complained about their submissiveness while taking advantage of it at every possible opportunity. He scowled at their "lack of initiative" while never offering any reason for them to use it. He whispered about their lack of tidiness, without explaining to them the standards he wished them to work towards. Everything about his style was adverse to their doing a good job. But he couldn't see it as his problem. Not yet.

Tomorrow, I needed to get him in a quiet room and try to learn more about his views. See where the beginning and hyper-extension of his attitudes were, look for the roots. I was always surprised by the amount of human psychology I needed for this job. Sometimes it was just about making the unconscious conscious, as they say. And draw out from him a better way to meet his own aims.

Nobody wanted to talk to me in my business class seat. No fellow passengers insistent on a chat. The unrushed flight attendant, offering a wide range of alcoholic drinks, asked me if I was having a nice day.

"Well," I replied, "it just got a whole lot better when I got to sit here instead of back there."

She dipped her head knowingly pouring my rum and coke (with a lime). "Know what you mean. I was bumped up too. Thought I'd be pouring 84 drinks instead of 16."

She handed me the drink with one hand, touching the back of my hand to steady it with her other. The warmth of her fingers on my skin felt good ... I wished it would stay warm like that for longer.

There was a lot more prep work to do before my workshops tomorrow. But when I got to my hotel room, I felt distracted, feisty. I had a shower, watched the news and laid down in bed. My skin felt soft and easy to touch. My hand fell between my legs and I thought of the man attached to the forearm in the cockpit, whoever he was. I imagined his eyes, interested in me, perceptive. Curious, but not for too long. He watched me, and I watched him. Our bodies moved easily around each other, working slowly, carefully.

I needed food. I went down to the restaurant and walked confidently to my table. I felt strong, smart, and, for the first time in years, a little sultry.

A businessman with blonde, voluminous hair ate alone in a booth near mine. I noticed how he watched me as I walked in. I put my laptop and purse on the table, sat down, and smiled, just a little. He looked a second time.

The chicken burritos tasted the same as they always did. The house merlot was better than usual. I reviewed my emails as I ate - staff meetings, expense claim forms, more newsletters. Then an email from Steve: conference in Australia, invitation for me to be a speaker after a Danish cross-cultural expert had to cancel for family reasons. October 21-23. "A wonderful opportunity to get the Anderson Bargh brand out of America and into the wider world. Please reply by Friday."

Exciting stuff. I quickly finished eating and headed back to my room. I had so much work to do.

The businessman lifted his head slightly as I passed.

Chapter 16

LOS ANGELES - CHICAGO
DEPARTS 3:05 PM
SEPTEMBER 9, 2022

Four days of intense work later, I Ubered to LAX, watching the office blocks of central Los Angeles passing upright like tall watchmen hoping to catch a glimpse of the distant sea, reaching ever higher with their glass and steel strength. I imagined the thousands of people working inside them, leaning onto their computers, answering phone calls with their headsets, negotiating deals of importance and banality.

Behind each of these transactions was something more - creatures with feelings and pasts, with biases and worries. The woman who goes to the restroom and, with her dress hiked up around her waist, thinks about the timing of her last period. The man listening to the cheesy music in the elevator, reminded of an old girlfriend, feeling, for a moment, the flutter of wings in his chest. The dad who rings home near the end of his workday, wishing he could figure out how to spend more time with his son, hoping that he's ok, that he isn't watching porn, that being a latchkey kid won't set into motion a series of events that will haunt him forever.

In those buildings, people talk about work and their lives, threading together relationships that may be fun or sour, rewarding or trite. A guy trying to grow a beard is told playfully that he looks "spunky" by an older female colleague – a new confidence sparks. A woman sells raffle tickets to raise money for her daughter's soccer trip, beginning a heated conversation about the modern demands of school sports. A boss reveals her husband has prostate cancer. A new line of empathy is formed.

Without even knowing it, colleagues become interwoven. Connected.

I passed building after building, vertical villages of networks and liaisons.

These days, most of my life is spent outside my own village. In all this travelling, my connections are only rehearsed, pre-determined. Temporary. Transactioned. T...

The seat next to mine on the plane was, unusually, empty. After take-off, I put my purse and laptop bag on the seat next to me, hoping the guy in the aisle seat wouldn't mind. It was another beautiful autumn day in LA – I could see through the thin cirrocumulus into the coppery California desert. I watched as we flew over small towns below, wondering who lived there. Why anyone would live there.

"Have you heard of the Dunbar number?" Sandra had asked.

I'd shaken my head as I topped up her California shiraz. "Nope, what's that?"

"The number of relationships that a human brain can manage. Any bigger, the clan becomes too hard to manage."

We'd been talking about socializing as we got older. Sandra could always pull out an academic nugget of information.

"Yeah, we're hard-wired to deal with an average of 150 relationships at a time, with an inner circle of 12. It has to do with the size of our neocortex, apparently. The bigger the volume of that region of the brain, the more social relationships we can cope with."

"I wonder how big yours is," I said from the stool of her fabulous breakfast bar. We always seemed to catch up at her place these days. Carl was never home anyway.

"And yours," she smiled, stunningly. "Prehistorically, if our clan's numbers exceeded what our neocortex could grapple with, relationships could become damaged or … neglected. Maybe conflicts were left unresolved, or groups of homo sapiens split or went to battle with each other. Our brain's social capabilities has boundaries, apparently."

"I see … are you saying that's why I'm a crap friend as I get older?" I teased.

"No! But I'm saying that maybe you're setting your expectations about your relationships too high. Maybe with all that work you do – all the people you deal with through work – your brain can only handle so much."

"Maybe. Or maybe I'm just becoming an ambivert as I head towards 50."

"What the fuck is an ambivert?" No one could swear with class like Sandra.

"An ambivert – not an introvert, not an extrovert, but an ambivert. You know, we can switch between both. So when I come home, I can't be fucked contacting my friends 'cause I've switched from people-person to," and here I paused and darkened my face, "to woman-of-the-cave."

"A chameleon of personality traits, of sorts."

"Yes." I flashed her a twisted smile, crossed my eyes, laughed, and knocked back another gulp of excellent wine.

I leaned my forehead against the plane window and counted my tribe in my head. Dottie, Dylan, Jess, Christopher, Sandra – do I have to include Carl in my intimate social group even though he's sort of a jerk? My friends Liz, Carla, maybe Lisa. Are we even supposed to count family members? Maybe "intimate" means "non-relative." Gosh, if it does, that's only Liz, Jess, Carla, Lisa … is Sandra related to me by marriage? Does she count?

For god's sake, if I can only count my inner circle of companions on one hand, maybe there's something wrong with me? Something wrong with my neocortex. I'm sure I can include, at least, my kids and dependent brother… surely.

I glanced down at my laptop on the seat next to me. There was so much to do on this flight home – notes to take about the LA work, plans for next week's trip to make. At least I didn't have to download any new emails in this Wi-Fi-free zone. A sanctuary from relentless communications. For now.

The cirrocumulus gave way to a thick blanket of cumulus. I stared into the whiteness as it glided below me, a smooth procession of enormous cauliflowers. Tiredness set in, deep and thick. Too heavy to lift.

I looked down at my laptop again. Then out to the cauliflowers. Could they sense my disconnect with myself, my people, my everything?

Chapter 17

CHICAGO – MIAMI

DEPARTS 7:55 AM

SEPTEMBER 12, 2022

Arlene was sitting Sphinx-like when I arrived at the office Monday morning. Her hands were folded on the reception desk in front of her, waiting for me.

"How you doing girl?" she growled in her raspy cigarette voice.

"Hey! Good to see you. Keeping everyone in line?"

"I'm a tryin'" she graveled, quicker than usual. "But that Australian thing has got us all jumping up and down. You better get on in there and see Steve – he knows you're comin'."

I sighed under my breath. It'd been nearly three weeks since I'd been at the head office, and I wanted to catch up with my colleagues.

"Oh boy oh boy," I feigned excitement. The conference was a rousing prospect, but we all knew that before a big event, there was always more work than hours in the workday. And on top of everything else. I could feel the tension building in my back already.

"Well, you just take your time then, girl," Arlene said slowly, her uncanny telepathy kicking in. "Steve's gotta wait his turn too."

I heeded her wise advice, talking to another consultant about his work and the inroads I was making in LA, goofing off with the guys in IT, and even nipping outside with Arlene on her break to watch her smoke and hear about her first grandchild. It always surprised me how youthful some grandmothers seemed since they and their kids started their reproductive lives at an age evolution favored. I'd been young-ish too when Dylan was born – 24 – but Arlene and her daughter had both been 18.

I finally knocked on Steve's door with a full cup of coffee in my hand; our talks were infrequent, and always long.

Steve and his crazy neckties. Today, it featured bright-red hot dogs hugged by cream-colored buns. He stood as I walked in, pulling the assortment of wieners to his chest.

"There she is!" he bellowed. "Recovered from your journeys yet?"

"Hardly had time, Steve." I said playfully. "You keep me working too much!"

I sat in the chair opposite his desk. My bottom sank into the soft cushion, confirming with thanks that it was not an airplane seat. Taking a long sip of coffee, I felt a sudden sense of satisfaction. Of, in fact, accomplishment.

"You sure are getting our name out there Cora. I was reading a magazine the other day and your name popped up, just like that. Something about fixing up some tensions out east. Or maybe it was down south - but it sure made me proud. And I'm glad they mentioned where you worked."

What Steve was missing in memory he made up for in warmth. His southern roots, even after 30 years in Chicago, had never been swept away by the northern winds.

"Well, thanks." Did I say "thanks" with a drawling 'A'? Accents can be catching. "I've had some really challenging projects and was able to try out some new stuff in the past couple of months. That Arizona State Press article came through the CEO of Marcus Pfeiffer. The company won a business award in Phoenix and he attributed some of the company's success to the work we've been doing there. I think I'll be able to replicate that work in their offices in Miami and Boston."

As "Miami and Boston" rolled off my tongue, I could smell the artificially air-freshened hallways of the hotel and taste the predictable ping of the chicken cordon bleu while seated in the ground floor restaurant. I shook these sensations off, returning to the nourishing heat of the coffee in my hands.

"I know you'll keep it up. Now," he adjusted his hot dog cornucopia across his chest yet again, "this conference – what's it? – ABD or something like that. In Sydney."

"The Australian Business Diversity Association."

"Looks like their keynote speaker –"

"Elise Madden"

"Know her?"

"Know of her. One of the best in the European cultural values space."

"Well, I know you'll fill in for her just fine. It's not a lot of notice, but our team will help. We've got uh, Janice on the resources, Greg is sending your information to the conference organizers, and Arlene will go ahead and book your tickets as soon as you get some time with her later today. This is a great opportunity for us, Cora, and I hope you can see that all the extra work will be worth the effort for an international event like this."

"For sure. Thanks for the help - I haven't even begun to put something together for the presentation yet."

"You'll get there. Now, tell me this: I know you've been as busy as a moth in a mitten lately. Why don't you take some time off while you're over there and look 'round Australia? When Joyce and I went there with the kids, we went up to Brisbane and saw sea turtles, and crocodiles. Whales even. How about you take some time for yourself and relax a little?"

"I was thinking the same thing. I could stop in New Zealand on the way back for a few days. I just need to see if I can postpone a couple of seminar dates in LA and Phoenix."

"New Zealand? I've always wanted to go there. Hear it's beautiful."

"My mom was from there. She came to college in Minnesota and met my dad there. Only child, so she broke my grandparents' hearts by moving so far away. "

"Sounds like it'll be a good vacation spot for you then."

I could see a natural segue emerging to raise a more pressing topic. I continued, "I have to say, I'm not sure how long I can keep this workload up. On one hand, it's kinda nice to have such a packed schedule, but on the other, my personal life is taking a hit."

A wrinkle appeared above his eyes. He nodded in concern.

"I'm really starting to feel the impact of the travel. You know, things like fitness and relationships, having downtime. My kids have felt it too, and you know about my brother Christopher. I wish I could just, like, get some more clients in Chicago rather than in other cities. And most weeks, I wish there could be two of me to help get through all the work."

"Maybe after this conference, there'll be more local clients. But that's not good, Cora." And then, as if he suddenly remembered a takeaway point from a management course said, "What can we do to help?"

"I've been thinking about training someone else up to assist. There are lower-level workshops that look set to continue across larger companies, like Marcus Pfeiffer. Once I set things up and develop the training programs, another experienced trainer could deliver it. I would supervise and monitor, but I don't have to physically be there to roll out these workshops. That would leave me more time to win more work."

Steve leaned back in his chair and looked out the window onto the adjacent building on Monroe St. "Agreed."

"What - that I don't have to be the one training, or that we can look at hiring someone else?"

"That you don't have to be the one training. It makes sense to get you some training support, but my question would be whether we contract someone in to undertake this work on an ad hoc basis, or if we have enough work to hire someone on a more permanent basis."

"I definitely have enough work to take someone on permanently, and that's what I really want." I looked down at my coffee cup, now lukewarm. "Steve, I'm really tired. I know having a break in New Zealand will help a little, but when I come back, I don't want things to be as hectic as they are now. I need an experienced trainer I can rely on to share my load."

I'd talked to Sandra about this work pressure last week, and she reminded me of the value of a subtle, friendly threat. "A hint," she'd said, "that if you don't get what you want, then there are several other consultancy firms that would be willing to provide it."

I looked at Steve carefully and could almost see the calculations going on behind his eyes: another mid-level employee at $1600 per week, $85K per year, plus overheads, resulting in $100k less profit per year, for how much more income? It was time to make my intentions clearer.

"I'll do the Australia conference and have a break," I said with as much confidence as I could muster. "Then, let's review it when I get back. I just want you to know that I can't carry on at this level of activity, and that we'll need to change something to make this work better for me. I love my work, you know that Steve, but I need to share the workload with specialists on a regular basis, not just buy it in when I can't cope with it all."

He nodded his head. His voice lowered authoritatively. "Let me think about it. I see where you come from. But I also have a business to run, staff to pay every week. Taking on another employee is not something I can do lightly. I'll need to look at your forecasted work." He rose from his chair, ready to end this conversation. "I'm sure you understand."

It was a start, anyway.

I walked with him to the door. As he reached to open it for me, he said, "Australia, eh? You really should think about getting up to Brisbane to see those critters. Joyce loved those giant turtles."

As I headed back to my desk, it wasn't sea creatures I was thinking of. I could hear the crack of the waves as I lay in Grandma and Grandpa's old bedroom. I could smell the snapper smoking on "the barbie." ready for friends to drop by to share. I could feel the titillation of opening the door to that room for the first time, to touch those things.

Miami started emerging in the landscape below. Gaps between the stratus clouds revealed suburbs, sparkling with swimming pool blue and the glare of sun on white roads. I liked this place. So would Christopher. I really should bring him here one day.

When I visited him this week, he'd immediately buried his head in my shoulder, wanting affection, saying nothing. I put both arms around him and squeezed hard, like Mom would have. I kissed his head, smelling his hair to make sure the caregivers were doing their jobs. He started rocking, then humming a little tune. Mom had always said that rocking was to Christopher like a barometer was to atmospheric pressure. If he started rocking himself, it was time to ease off some pressure. Or make a change.

"There's nothing to do today, Cora," he said thoughtfully. "Nothing to do today."

My eyes welled with tears, and I continued to rock him, rock us, connected in a single unit by arms and genes and everything else.

Christopher deserved a fuller life, a life with more people, more purpose, more experiences. But I didn't know how to make that happen. I'd done what I could since our parents died. Carl had been useless. I felt that what I'd done, the way I'd set things up for Christopher, wasn't enough. Why should his life, with that infectious spirit and yet plenty of limitations, be made up of only board games, movies and an occasional visit to the zoo?

The plane lowered smoothly toward the never-ending summer of Miami, despite it being autumn in the rest of the country. I watched the earth draw nearer, considering Christopher's fate.

Then, that other person in my life who needs me right now: Dottie.

Dottie had grown into a roaming, angry woman who, like Christopher, sent me barometric signals that things weren't right in her world.

She wasn't always that way.

At her sixth birthday party, when her friend Seymour wet his pants during Pin the Tail on the Donkey, Dottie had taken his hand and led him quietly into her bedroom to change. As an eight-year-old, her hair growing in flattering locks down her shoulders, I would take her cheeks into both my hands and inspect her face in the metamorphosis of her youth, her clear eyes holding mine in a ray of shared admiration. Then, I saw her leave for high school in the morning, those same cheeks dotted with red bumps, then covered with brown foundation and concealer, feeling her frustration, hoping that acne wouldn't cover up her determined, knowing lifeforce.

She'd come to dinner on Sunday night, for the first time in weeks. Her black clothes hung loosely over her thin frame and her shirt covered, as usual, the insides of her forearms. I guess some stories don't need to be told.

She hadn't asked for money for a while and was working again. Some comic book shop in Lakeview. That had to be good enough, for now.

I made the mistake of asking what the other people in the shop were like. Students? Artists? Comic book enthusiasts?

"Why do you even care, Mom? What's that got to do with anything?"

"Just asking," I said, hoping to divert an argument.

"You're always wanting me to be someone I'm not. All you care about is me having a stable job and being around the right sorts of people. The people I work with are like, fine, OK?"

"OK." I scooped some more nachos into my mouth and looked to Dylan for a way out. He looked down at the table, then over to Janey.

"For fuck's sake," Dottie nodded into her meal.

"Dottie!" At least I could still reprimand her for swearing at the dinner table.

Silence. The sound of corn chips being crunched.

The wheels moaned loudly as they hit the runway. Miami. Again.

Chapter 18

Maroa Bay
Thursday, 27 October 2022

As much as I loved the flood of memories and sensations, squatting in my special room for most of the day made my knees ache. By late afternoon, I needed to stretch my legs and see the clouds.

I paced quickly along the length of the beach, watching two clouds move undecidedly around each other in a sort of circular dance.

When I got to that place where the boulders outnumber the stretches of sand, I looped around a dark rock and headed back towards the other end of the beach. For a cloudy weekday, it was unusually busy. Three dogs ran in circles chasing each other as their people discussed their breeds; an elderly couple marched side-by-side along the high tide line; a young family of four that I'd noticed on the beach earlier in the week played near the water's edge. What did they do to support this lifestyle:

work from home? Independently wealthy? Taking a year off from their corporate jobs for a bohemian stint?

A man walked barefoot along the water's edge, stopping to talk to the young family. He bent down to speak to the toddlers, eliciting some happy reaction. As I approached, he looked up at me, nodding his head once with a smile.

Tama. My pulse quickened.

"Kia ora!" I said cheerfully, remembering to roll my 'r'. "How are you and what are you doing here?" Stop blurting out a bunch of stuff all at once. Calm down Cora.

"Hey hey," he said, ignoring my questions and instead, touched the sandy cheek of one of the toddlers as he rose. He casually put his hands in his pockets and stepped towards me.

"Funny to see you again," I said, trying to keep it Kiwi-casual not American-enthusiastic.

"Small place, New Zealand, eh?" he smiled.

"What have you been up to? Did you stay in the pool for much longer after I left?" That's two questions Cora. Damn it, slow down.

"Yeah, nah I saw a big fat kererū, then headed home," he said with patient spaces between his words. "What about you – been enjoying your holiday?"

He started to saunter just above the water line on the hard sand left by the outgoing tide. I followed alongside. "It's been great – lots of walks and down time and oh yeah – I stopped at

Tairua on the way back from Tita Beach the other day. Wow, that place sure has changed since I was last there!"

Tama snickered softly. "Yeah. There's a lot of that sort of thing happening here. It's all changing, eh?"

We both looked out to the headland as we walked. The sea breeze ruffled our hair. I wanted to launch into spoken words, but I knew I needed to get better at just being quiet and taking in the landscape.

The angle of the waves differed slightly from the previous day as they approached the headland. A cumulus nimbus kept blocking then unblocking the sun.

Tama bent down to pick up a whole paua shell – a mollusk with a shimmering iridescent shell – and polished its purply inside with the bottom of his t-shirt as he walked.

After what seemed to me like long moments of silence, I looked to the northern end of the beach and remembered something.

"I meant to ask you the other day," I said, walking a bit closer to him. "You mentioned how some of your people were at war with each other at first and then when the settlers came, they got involved in some trouble. Have you ever heard the story about a white settler who was involved in a bunch of murders on this beach?"

"Nah," Tama said shaking his head. "None of my people fought around here. It was usually up in the hills up above 'cos that's where the pā was, where they lived."

"OK. I met this guy on a plane once who was from Tita Bay and he said that when he was a kid, they never came to the north end of Maroa beach because they thought it was cursed. This guy called Dicky Bane went nuts one night and killed a bunch of people, right here."

"Nah, mate. If something that big had happened, I'd know about it. Maybe your fella's got his stories mixed up a bit, eh?"

The block in my gut thickened, gnawing, almost bulging as he spoke. I needed something else to talk about.

"How's the landscaping going?"

"Landscaping? More like mowing, mate. Just doing a ton of houses that the Jafas only use once in a while."

"Jafas?"

"Just Another Friggin' Aucklander. They're everywhere," he said, laughing warmly.

I smiled at the sand. My grandparents and mom would've been three of those.

"But mostly I help on the marae. Always planting. Bringing kai for the oldies. Whatever the aunties need help with. That kinda thing. And I gotta look after the urupā 'cos the weeds get too high there around the graves."

"Where's the marae?"

"Pukepaukena. Overlooks the main road and faces out to sea. Pākehā call it Pumpkin Hill for some strange reason."

Pākehā, that's right. White folk, like me. "Oh yeah, does it sit up there on a hill on the left as you head north out of Tairua?"

"Yeah, that's it."

"I've noticed it before. But I'm usually driving, so haven't taken a good look. Beautiful place though."

"True. God's own. Te toto o te tangata he kai, te oranga o te tangata, he whenua, he oneone."

I waited for him to translate. Not too fast Cora. After what seemed like many seconds, I finally said "What does that mean?"

"Food gives us the blood in our bodies, but our health comes from the land. And from the soil."

"Hmm," was the only word that I could conjure.

We walked past the parking lot and were heading towards my end of the beach. I didn't want Tama's easy company to end.

"Want to pop in for a hot tea or a coffee – I mean – a cuppa? I'm just right there," I said, pointing to the bach.

"Hey hey – now there's a good spot. Right on the beach, eh?"

"Yeah, pretty lucky I know. So …"

"Sure, I'll come in for a cuppa. I usually only get to see the outsides of places like this, eh, so it'll be good to see how the other half lives," he joked.

"Keep your expectations low!" I said, heading towards the door.

As I opened the cupboard doors and switched the kettle on, I sensed Tama watching me. But when I turned around, his eyes were scanning the horizon again. I set the cup of tea down on the table in front of him.

"At your marae, and when you're helping out with everything there, do you, like, get paid?"

Tama chortled slightly. "Nah, it's not like that. You just gotta do your part. Everyone just helps in their own way. It's hard to explain to a ..."

"Pākehā?"

I liked the gentle response in his nod.

"But – what if you need groceries or to pay bills or something? What if you can't help out?"

"Then we get kai and we find koha to share around. It's the old ways, you know? It's not this 'everyone's out for himself' thing. We're part of the same, like, a group, a family, you know. We go way back. If someone needs something, then we just figure out how to get it for them. So, I'm like, not going to go hungry or nothing like that."

Grandma would've been into that. A great example of collectivist communities living within an individualistic Western country. Maybe I could use it to demonstrate in my workshops how individualistic vs collectivist societies weren't necessarily at opposite ends of the same cultural continuum, and that, like plenty of the post-Hofstede research argued, they were more nuanced than that, layered by geography, multiple value systems, and colonizing forces. Stop Cora. Just stop.

"You're from Chicago, right?"

"Yep. Ever been there?"

"Nah. Never left the North Island. Guess I got everything I need right here," Tama smiled, satisfied.

I was slightly distracted by Tama's waist as he stretched out over the back of the chair. I imagined him lying on his back in my bed, abdomen flat and wide chest sprawling out like an unexplored beach before me.

"Chicago's a great place to live," I said. "Windy and sometimes cold, but there's a lot going on there. I love it."

"Your kinda town."

"My kinda town." We stared knowingly at each other for a moment, heads bobbing gently up and down. There it was. That connection.

"Let's go for a swim," he grinned, without moving his eyes from mine.

I looked out to the beach. "It's not exactly swimming weather, is it?"

"All weather is swimming weather," he said, knocking back the rest of his cuppa. He stood up and stretched his arms up into the air. "Besides, it's nearly dusk and we might see the colors change in the sky if that cloud buggers off."

"Yeah, but I don't –"

"A different wahine – remember? You'll feel like a different woman after a good sunset swim." I felt, in a playful way, there was little choice. When he headed towards the stairs, he called back to me, "I'm just gonna grab my togs and towel from the car. Back in a sec."

What the heck - I could use the company and certainly a swim. Besides, here I was on vacation in Maroa. Tama was nice.

I walked into my bedroom and changed into my swimsuit, tidying up a few of the clothes on the floor and straightening the duvet covers.

As my feet hit the sand, I felt a rush of wind brush past me, an aftersmell naturally clean but oily, mixed with mint or eucalyptus. Tama ran into the low waves and, as soon as the sea was up to his thighs, dove into the water. He stayed under for a long time. My entry was much slower. When the cold waves slapped against my knees, I saw a wet head pop up just a couple of yards away.

"Come on," he said confidently, stretching out his hand to me. "Let's head out to the headlands."

*

Bryce had always taken the lead. I would respond, marionette-like, to any sexual twitch of his muscles or signal for things to move in a certain direction. It frequently did. Tom and I, even in our youth and dragged down by pregnancies and his emerging alcoholism, didn't have as lively a sex life. But my sex life with Bryce was dictated, for the most part, by my younger lover.

With Tama, I sensed there was a respect, a line of authority, that he wouldn't cross without my clear invitation.

It was nearly dark when we walked up the beach towards the bach, our towels draped loosely around our shoulders. Our bodies kept brushing each other, as if their general direction of travel was pulling into the same flight path, bumping lightly, vying for the same space. We chatted about the auburns we'd seen in the sun-setting sky, the hidden eddy we'd found, and the trickery of distance – the headlands were in fact closer than they'd at first seemed in that early evening light. Starting off, we'd swum vigorously with wide breast strokes and strong kicks, calming to relaxed paddles as we approached the headland.

When we got inside the bach, Tama waited for me to invite him up. "Shower?" I said with what may've been a hint of flirtation. It had been a while. My skills, dulled.

"Sweet as," he said, and followed me up the stairs. As I leaned into the shower to show him the exact position of the shower nozzle for a perfect temperature, he leaned in too, pressing his tattooed shoulder against my arm. I brought my free hand to rest on it and said "OK?" Maybe my brow arched. I don't know.

But I did know it was time to bring an afternoon of foreplay to an end.

Tama took a step into the shower and stood up tall. We were now facing each other in a waterless shower in our cold swimsuits. His hand touched my waist lightly. "Why don't you show me?" he said firmly, looking straight at me. It wasn't the first time I'd noticed how bright the whites of his eyes were. Unpatterned. Unrivered. Unflinching.

I giggled a little, reaching up to point the shower head away so that the initial cold spurt was away from us. But when I lifted the nozzle, the pipes vibrated loudly, gargled, then ejaculated a sudden spurt. Tama laughed in a low voice as cold water fanned our skin. Shivering in unison, I laughed too until, finally, I rested my forehead on his shoulder.

Now that I was so close to it, I touched the place I'd been admiring since I met him. Where the fronds of ink ended against his collarbone, there was a deep notch. Throughout the day, I'd noticed that the skin in this indentation seemed to pulse with Tama's emotions – rolling as he laughed, throbbing as he recovered from exercise, shimmering as he looked across the sea. Now, I stroked my finger across it, wondering how that notch might respond to what was about to happen.

The water now streamed out in straight, warm lines. As I reached up to aim the shower head down, Tama spun me around so that its warmth struck me first. I tilted my flattened hair back under the spray as he wound both his hands around my neck, kissing me with thick, warm lips.

A new scent filled the shower. The heat opened our pores and at last the full fragrance of the man could be enjoyed: oily with lust, mossy like the forest's floor, of sage and sea salt.

 The wet swimsuits ended up on the bathroom rug. The hot water heater, never big enough for an entire houseful of people, ran out of steam before we did. As the water turned from hot to warm, from warm to tepid, I called into the night with a primal sound, full of the surge of the powerful waves that we had just swum in.

In one moment, I watched the indentation around Tama's collarbone move in waves, as if the rhythm of the sea lived inside him.

*

"You gonna come back here Cora, or is this it for you and this old place?" Tama was leaning over the fried fish and chips piled on a splay of paper on the Formica table, dipping thick French fries into a small, opened can of ketchup. Kiwis called it "tomato sauce." Come to think of it, that made more literal sense than "ketchup."

When he picked up the takeaways, Tama had stopped by the little grocery store and bought a few beers too.

I leaned back in my chair and took a sip, more relaxed than I'd remembered feeling in a very long time. The moon was shining a perfectly angular ray of light across the calm water. I felt, quite urgently, like saying stuff.

"I've been coming here all my life. My granddad built this place out of bits of leftover construction material and this and that he picked up along the way. My parents kept it going so we could have these incredible family vacations here – even though we lived so far away. They settled in Chicago, but my mom's from Auckland. This place was always our place, you know, that place that makes you feel…"

Tama waited, then offered a word, firm, but not pushy. "Strong?"

"Yes, I guess it does that to me."

"Yeah," he now looked out the window too. "We call that turangawaewae – the place where you stand. That's my marae for me, my people's land."

"That's a word my grandma taught me! 'Two-ranga-why-why' – I remember her saying that – yeah – and that for her it was here on this beach."

"Your gran Māori?"

"Scottish mostly."

"What about Chicago? You got connections with the land there too, eh?"

"Yeah, of course I do. I've spent a lot of time on the waterfront there – along Lake Michigan … it's so beautiful and powerful and it's on the edge of this magnificent city … it's always energized me. But the problem there is that I have to share it with so many people – literally millions. Here, it's so small and untouched that it seems easier, somehow, to feel its power."

He nodded slowly, not dropping his gaze from mine. He asked "But what about your history? Where do your people come from and … and why don't you go there to experience that?"

I thought about my dad's side of the family in Schaumberg, a suburb west of Chicago. Grandma Sumberland had gnarled fingers and a stooped back; as a girl, I was kind of scared of her. I remember Christopher announcing on the drive to her place once that she "looks like the witch in the Wizard of Oz!" I couldn't really see any meaningful connection to that place, other than where we had to go on Easter Sundays after church to have overcooked roast chicken and soggy peas.

My place? After the kids were born, it was probably here, with Tom. I could intuitively feel the intergenerational connection with a beach and a house and a village. But really, if I was honest with myself, I'd never really thought about a place that makes me feel strong.

It hurt my head a little to think about this, so I took another drink of strong Kiwi beer and popped a few chips in my mouth. Tama watched me carefully, looking a little uncertain, before speaking.

"This land where the house is, this place - it's worth a fortune now. There's heaps of rich Aucklanders and big companies that want to buy up places like this, right on the beachfront. You gonna do that too?"

"Don't know," I said, more honestly than I'd intended. "Marilen asked me about this the other day too. You know Marilen Hoskings, a property manager around here?"

"Think so – she the one that always wears flowery dresses and hats and stuff?"

"That's her."

"Yeah. Nice lady."

"She's kind of wanting us to sell up to that big hotel chain that wants to build here, but I don't know. My brothers and I could definitely use the cash right now, but it's not something we'd take lightly after it's been in the family for – what? – three generations now."

"Too right. Our marae's been here for 16 generations. And there's no way any of us could sell that off … it's bigger than that." He quickly added "Mind you, our whānau is pretty broke so we sure could use the dosh!"

I looked away from him then. In the spreadsheet of our short-lived relationship, money belonged in an entirely different column from our feelings about the land. Something felt wrong and I didn't want to go there.

I leaned forward across the table and said mischievously, "Check out that moonlight – wanna go for a walk on the beach?"

Shoulder to shoulder, we didn't pretend this time that we didn't want our flight paths to cross as we walked along the dark beach. The families and retirees were all gone, the waves lapped gently at our bare feet, and the light from the half-moon danced across our faces with its celestial magic.

I looped my hand in his. It was nice being with someone else and not following, not leading, but just walking alongside them as they are, in that moment and no other. When we got to the end of the beach near the boulders, Tama turned at the same spot where I usually spun around to walk the other way. He stopped for a moment, took both my hands and faced me in the mildness of the light. The sea breeze pushed his dark waves of hair across his cheek.

"Tenā koe Cora. Me te mea ko Kōpū ka rere i te pae."

I didn't know what it meant but it felt strong, and right. We drew together, working our hands along the silhouettes of our bodies, touching abdomens, pressing noses, rubbing cheeks. Maybe it was near the same spot that Tom and I had circled each other in the new rain 25 years before. Maybe it was a place that my own mother had kissed my dad. Maybe it was only for a moment, but our strands of connections, the exchange of electricity I needed to power my life, were, right then, on fire.

Interstice

Above Maroa Bay
27 October 2022

During a heavy dew or rain we hold tight to your building's overhangs and clutch onto your school windows and laugh as we watch you try to explain the water cycle

   Yes we move in cycles that shape us into different patterns Forces loosen and tighten our connections they tilt us downwards by the falling coolness Others lift back towards the hills and mountains Upwards some reflect the light then begin their tireless journeys northwards towards the equator while others break upwards into gas yielding to the forces of the earth's rotation Those spinning above the known atmospheres above winds and gravity are re-shaped into water droplets heading down Down to the tips of new grass then indentations in the earth then gullies then streams and eventually out to sea to begin their journeys again

But that is only half of it There is more to us than that There are other forces unknown to you that bind us and drive us apart

You must feel them too

Today we watch a woman who faces towards us Curious and seeking answers Sky-facer observes us as we drift towards her jostling for position

To her we may look like the spokes of a wheel or the rays of a star as if there were some unseen central energy forcing everything else out from it in bursts of outward rows

To us we see two people like droplets like molecules brought together by heat and light

Sky-facer's and the man's energy is at first tenuous As they move along the sand it thickens by new pressures Powers that unite them Forces that drive them apart

Chapter 19

```
PITTSBURGH - CHICAGO
DEPARTS 2:47 PM
OCTOBER 5, 2022
```

It was Sandra who told me first. She could hardly speak. When I first picked up my phone, all I could hear was lots of breathing and a couple of soft whimpers. Once her tears slowed, the words came fast. "Years of debt" and "fucking idiot" in between "bad crypto currency" and "they're going to take our house."

Ancient instincts kicked in as I listened to my sister-in-law, more friend than relative. I needed to protect the ones I loved from the destructive forces around them, bring calm to their storms. But this time, the storm was my brother. Which of the two parties do I protect? The one with biological ties or the one with emotional ones? Which trumps which?

"What can I do, Sandra?" I asked. "Should I ring Carl, should I go to my bank? Can I try to intervene in the court order?"

"Nothing!" she nearly shouted, letting go of the grace that she so naturally exuded. "There's nothing you can do to fix this, Cora! Just ring your brother and tell him not to come home. I've had enough!"

Deep down, it surprised me that it had taken her so long to get to this point. I knew I needed to walk a fine line between support for her complaints and empathy for the man that she would probably end up resolving the problem with. As Mom used to say, "I don't want to know about your spats with your boyfriend/husband, because you'll go and make up, in bed or somewhere else, and I'll be left behind thinking how angry I am at him."

But this was different. Sandra's inconsolable, bitter shift in response to Carl's wrongdoings left me certain that this was no temporary conflict, but rather the final escalation in a long marriage of coping with behaviors she didn't understand or want to know about. Her life as a music instructor and an active supporter of the arts community in west Chicago was comfortably isolated from Carl's cutthroat, hard-nosed world of international banking. This recent news threatened to disrupt everything they'd built together: relationships, reputations, assets, their shared future.

I knew this as I breathed into the phone, trying to conjure up the calm that Sandra had often used in response to the dramas of my own life. A part of me wanted to tell Sandra to leave my brother, that her life would be better off, in the long run, without him. But another part of me wanted to remind her that even in our darkest, lowest days, all of us are worth loving.

"I should've seen it coming," called Sandra's voice into my hotel room. "The absences, the unanswered questions, the, the – I try to just get on with my own life and let Carl do his own thing, but his inability to talk about any aspect of his work should've set off alarm bells years ago. He's been knee-deep for ages – what the fuck was I thinking?!"

"Sandra, it's not your job to do Carl's thinking for him. He makes his own decisions, and you make yours. Please don't take responsibility for any of the stupid decisions my brother's made."

"And that's the other thing, he's your brother." She pulled away from the phone to gulp back more tears. "This must be so hard for you and I'm really sorry. I shouldn't really even be talking to you about this now. God - he's your brother!"

"Yes, you should, Sandra, you should. We're bigger than – we're more than that, you know that. We're friends. Old friends."

But even as I spoke, I thought: what would I do if she left? Would we – could we – still be close?

Then, it became clear what I needed to do.

"I'm going to hang up and ring Carl now. I need to hear from him what's going on. But first, I need to know: where are you and will you be ok?"

She took a moment before she could speak. "At home. Yes, I'll cool off now." Then added more lightly, "I'm going to ring my sister. Maybe for once she'll let me talk about my own problems instead of hers."

"Good girl. I'm going to call you back later tonight – I'm in Pittsburgh but I'll give you a call as soon as I can, OK?"

*

A kid moved down the aisle with a large backpack on, twice the width of his own body. His pack crashed into the aisle seat in the row in front of mine and, with his closely shaven head atop two wide, wandering eyes, he pointed at the middle seat and shouted in a European language, "Daar is het!" Dutch? German? Probably Dutch.

I smiled a Companionable Cora smile at him and his bespectacled father, who helped him slip off his backpack and heave it into the overhead locker. I looked out on the Pittsburgh Airport runway lined with smaller regional planes, wondering if people were less likely to leave personal items on smaller planes when they exited. Just wondering.

Last night, I was surprised that Carl had picked up his phone immediately when I called. His voice was different. I could hear straight away that something had shifted.

"I don't know what to say," he said, when I explained that Sandra had called me. "There's no reason or excuse or anything, Cora. It was a stupid gamble, that's all. And I lost."

I resisted the instinct to count how many times I'd heard Carl utter the words "stupid" or "lost" about his own actions. Close to zero. Self-importance meant his humility was rare.

"How bad did you lose, Carl?" I asked in a sisterly tone. "Sandra thinks they're going to take your house."

"I sunk a lot – a million or more – into it. But to be honest, things hadn't been going my way before that either. The financial downturn, the pandemic, it didn't play well into our investments."

There he was, I thought. The Carl that blamed outside forces for his failings, never himself. To my amazement, that attitude didn't last long.

"That's not to say I didn't fuck up, Cora. I did. I kept making risky decisions with my clients' assets for too long. I kept thinking it'd recover. It'd bounce back. It always does. But this time," and I heard his voice squeak when he said this, "it fucking didn't."

"I thought you were working for Mastercard or a big bank, don't they have, like, insurance or something for these situations?"

"It's not that work. I kept some of my private clients. Probably shouldn't have. But anyway - shit. Sandra. Can you talk to her? I don't know what to do. She's – she's …"

"Had enough?"

"Yeah, I guess you could say that. I understand. She works so hard and does so much for us and for everyone else. She just wants a normal relationship and some, you know, certainty. She doesn't need this, and I'd be lost, lost without her. You know that, Cora."

There was only one other time in my life, decades ago, when Carl spoke to me in those same pleading, vulnerable terms. Mom had just died, Dad was a 50-odd-year-old basket case, and as the last woman standing in our immediate family, I seemed to get the lion's share of family problems that required even a flicker of emotional intelligence. Carl was, like the rest of us, grieving, young, and bobbing around trying to figure out what his twenty-something self should do with the rest of his life. His long-time girlfriend had unexpectedly dumped him, and he'd asked me, one drunken night out, why.

"But she said she loved me," he cried in a dark bar up around Lincoln and Halsted. With his handsome face screwed up in ways that I'd never seen before – twisted, tired, toiled – he'd asked imploringly, "doesn't she know what we're going through right now?"

Nearly twenty years later, that same need for help resounded in his voice. A plea for help. His marriage, and his comfortable life, were now at stake.

"How much, Carl? How much are we talking about to get you out of this mess? Just tell me, straight up, no bullshit: how big is this problem?"

I heard an intake of breath. Good. Air is good in these situations. As he exhaled, he said "If I could raise some funds right now, I could go to some friends and see what they could do." He spoke more deeply now.

"Then, with a small deposit of say, five or 10 percent, I could probably get a secured loan on the house and our assets and borrow the rest." Like a towering cumulus gaining force as it lifted, I could hear the pressure rise in his words. "Yes. Archie might help. I'll call him."

"What is five to 10 percent of the debt? What is it, Carl?"

"Tens of thousands." He slipped into a fragile voice again.

"How many? I may be able to help."

He hated this. His younger sister, the solo mother who was always trying to make it on her own in spite of her parade of failed relationships, the one he had bossed, and mocked, and bullied around in our childhood, now offering to help him out of the shitstorm of his life.

"Ten, maybe fifteen," he said, reluctantly.

"You mean, ten or fifteen tens of thousands, right? So, like, $150,000?"

"Yeah, about that."

"And that might get you out of the immediate debt. You could go to a bank for the rest?"

"Maybe. Maybe not a bank but some other lender. Yes, Cora. I think so."

"Ok."

He paused, pregnantly. Pulsingly. Then said quietly, "I'm sorry."

"I know, Carl. I know you are."

"But –" he stopped talking and breathing for a long while. "But Sandra – I – she just can't –"

"I know. It'll be OK. I'll talk to her."

"Will you?"

"Yes, tonight."

I flopped back on the hotel bed with a grunt. Anger. Resentment. Thick and strong. Maybe even revenge, like karma had finally circled back. Then came pity, sadness, even grief.

If our parents were alive, maybe we wouldn't both be such anchorless, drifting souls. Struggling to find ground in our turbulent world. Mom and Dad would've brought more insight into Carl's choices. All I was able to bring was a loan, and not even much of one.

The European boy in the seat next to me sat upright as the plane lurched forward towards Chicago. He scratched one spot in his shaven head as if a mosquito had made a home there, yet there was no sign, upon my quick inspection, of infestation. He spoke to his dad; I could make out every ninth word: *moeder, huis, verjaardag.* Something about a birthday. And his mom.

As the Ohio hills rolled along below us, I smoothed my fingers across a die I'd found in the restaurant at the Pittsburgh hotel, thinking about Carl, his beautiful wife, their kitchen's thick marble countertops, and my own role in all this.

The clouds, this time, told me nothing. I looked for shapes and patterns, some hint of pressure that would spark an insight or memories of cloud wisdom from Grandma. But they were just massive clusters of water droplets moving across the water cycle in white shapes, one after the other, connected by invisible forces.

No magic, no wisdom, no nothing.

Chapter 20

Maroa Bay
Friday, 28 October 2022

The morning light pushed past the curtains with unusual intensity. It would be, finally, a hot day. I rolled over and flung my arm across the bed, expecting it to settle across the chest of a man. But it landed on the mattress like a pancake on a plate.

I replayed the way we'd moved up the stairs with my back pressing against the edges, Tama's hands at once forcing my back upwards as he thrust into me, a satisfying force in every part of me and all at the same time. When I felt the soft mattress against my back, I'd pulled away from it and climbed on top of him. The last thing I remembered was the smell of the sea on his chest as I fell asleep against it.

I threw off the covers and shook my hair from my face. Hopefully Tama had found the coffee and eggs. I took a quick pee and threw on an oversized t-shirt as I headed into the kitchen. It was quiet, no sign of breakfast or even a hot drink.

A white piece of paper was folded cleanly and placed on its ends in the middle of the table, like a lighthouse. A warning to beware.

My body reacted first, sending me back towards the hall as if pushed by an unseeable fist. A hand clasped my tummy. I shouldn't have been so surprised. I knew this routine. It had happened before.

Tom's exit from my life had been traumatic. Simon's exit was of my own making. But Bryce's departure was a punch in the guts; a black swan of an event with no sign it was coming.

Other than an occasional dreamy, distant look towards the horizon or away from me, there was little in Bryce's behavior that suggested what was about to happen. He'd always been a roamer, never fitted into the landscape of urban life, never aspired for the professional goals that my friends and I did. He was an outlier and that's what I loved about him. He'd never expected me to be or do what other men in my life had. It excited me that he didn't attend work functions or many family gatherings; he was my own secret room of treasures that I alone got to come home to.

When we made love, we left everything about ourselves in another room. We met as equals, connecting with no consequences or expectations. I lived in my sphere of professional and family life, and he lived in his with his gym friends and mini adventures. It worked. It worked for two years.

One April day I woke up to find a note, standing like a sentinel in the middle of my oak table. Some impressive words that I'd never heard Bryce use before were on it: not wanting to feel "bound by the relationship" or made to feel "older than I am." After all we'd done together, after all our shared times, I was more alarmed by the end of that relationship than I had been with Tom and Simon. This time, it was my own emotions that had been caught by surprise.

Now, on the other side of the planet, there was another table. A letter at its center. Folded with its edge pointing with crisp innocence to the ceiling, its open edge waiting to reveal another rejection. A part of me dreaded reading it. Another part of me couldn't resist.

Whatever it said, this letter would go in a sacred place in my favorite room. In the shadowy back hall, past the jars and the toys, just after the corner turn, was a cardboard shoe box Dottie had decorated as a child. Smiley-faced stickers were encircled with her uneven hand-drawn lines. The letters of the alphabet were scattered like freckles between the stickers. I remember remarking on the neatness of her handwriting, to which she replied, importantly, "that's the way it's supposed to look, Mommy." Her reverence for rules seems to have waned over the years.

The box included Mom's last handwritten letter to me before she died, with its descriptions of her daffodils popping to life in early spring, Dad's latest fishing trip, and her subtle questions about when our next visit might be. Next to that letter were many more: Jess' adolescent rantings when she went to summer camp in her sophomore year ... a letter of acceptance from University of Wisconsin's Master's program, which I declined after learning I was pregnant with Dylan ... Bryce's departure letter was in there too.

Tama's could sit fittingly next to it.

I walked over to the kitchen window, turned the kettle on, and looked out to the sea. Above the horizon, cumulus clouds bubbled upwards like a volcano exploding in slow motion. What did they think of all this human silliness?

The gurgle of water in the kettle warmed my ears, pulling me inwards, to my kids, to my house in Lincoln Park, to Jess' laughter. Then, to a warmth that stirred in my belly, moving down between my legs, where Tama had opened a door that had for too long been shut.

I poured myself a cuppa, poking the tea bag with short stabs of the spoon.

It was big-girl time, Cora. What did you think? That you were going to have a happily-ever-after with your new lover in New Zealand? Really?

I looked back at the letter on the table. Exhaled. Sat down. Took a sip of sweet tea.

Underneath the A-framed paper were two things: a paua shell, polished so well that its striking purple and green wavey lines seemed to move as I turned it, and a beautiful feather, iridescent blue tipped with bronze. I inspected both in the morning light, admiring their natural sheen and traces of emerald, then stroking my fingers into the curve of the shell again, and again. I wondered which of New Zealand's native birds the feather had come from. Maybe a Tūī? Grandma would know. Tama too.

His handwriting was block-like, unlinked.

Cora – It didn't feel good to hang around. You were different than I thought you'd be. I shouldn't be here. My cuzzie from Auckland put me up to it. Works in some flash firm there. I don't know. It just doesn't make sense. I'm not saying nothing to him about you – I don't understand what he's up to. I had to get away - its whakama. But it wasn't like that for me. I'm sorry. It wasn't like that for me.

Tama

I could hear him speaking the words in my head. Low, firm, gentle words with a high note of worry, a dissonance in his background tone. I read them again. This time, I stopped on "whakama." I grabbed my phone – what does that even mean? Google Translate took its time. I watched the swirl of doom on the screen and thought – Tama, what's your cousin got to do with us and what the hell were you supposed to tell him about me?

A sharp knock jerked my rounded shoulders up. The door. My heart paced in sync with my feet as I dashed down the stairs.

But it wasn't him.

Marilen's face was more ashen than usual; the rosiness of her dress wasn't, for once, reflected in her cheeks. Maybe my face was different too. I realized then that I had nothing on but a big t-shirt – no undies, the fragrance of Tama trapped between my thighs and the shirt.

"Marilen, come in," I said as cheerfully as I could rally. "Sorry but, I'm still in my pajamas!"

"No worries – sorry I should've left it a bit later lovey."

"Coffee?"

"No thanks sweetie I'm just here for a sec," she said uncomfortably. I felt relieved – I didn't need company right now.

"It's just that the developers have been in touch with me this morning."

"Yeah?"

"And they asked me to come and speak with you."

"OK."

Marilen talked mostly to my chest, only casting her gaze to my eyes every few seconds, as if the words she was looking for were inked just above my cleavage.

"They - there's a deadline on their offer. Apparently things have been held up a long time by the local iwi and the resource consent expires next week."

"Why?"

"Not sure, but if they don't get everyone to agree on the development in the next week or so, the entire deal will have to go to the High Court and will probably take years to sort out. So they're pretty keen on getting a response from you ASAP."

"Wait. So, who's agreed to the development? Is everyone in Maroa Bay on their side?"

"Everyone who owns a property at this end of the beach is. Except –" she now glanced up at my eyes.

"– me?"

"Right."

"But you know I can't make a decision for my brothers at such short notice. This place is all of ours and – "

"Cora," Marilen's voice was different. Deeper. It didn't match her wardrobe.

"Hmm?"

"Carl has agreed. The decision – yours and Christopher's – is entirely your own."

"Carl has –"

"Yes," she spoke confidently now. "They've contacted him in Chicago. He's in the process of signing an affidavit to clarify his intentions."

Of course he is. Carl needs this to happen. Of course.

I puffed my chest out as it filled with air, then lowered it. I looked at the floor, half-expecting to see a blob of stressful ooze melting to the ground. Marilen folded her hands and placed her foot to one side, as if balancing herself. My thoughts came in quick succession: money, Christopher, Dottie, money, my secret room, Grandpa, Grandma, my own business, Dylan, Sandra ... in that millisecond, I could even feel Tama's hands on my hip bones, warm, glove-like.

"It sounds like EcoWorld, or whatever they're called, it sounds like they want this to happen this week. Have they got an offer price yet?"

As I spoke, another, recently neglected sentiment came. I thought of them all: the orange silk lady, the Māori guy from Tita Beach, the girl espousing Easton Institute's virtues – had their stories led me here, to this moment, to a decision that was now mine alone, but that would affect generations to come?

Or, have I merely woven together meaning in the stories of strangers? In a world of disconnect, have I connected the unrelated meanderings of those I spent a few intimate moments on planes with into a larger story?

"Yes Cora. They do." Something in her voice told me there was more at stake here than new growth for her region.

EcoWorld had a stake in Marilen too.

"It's nearly three million US dollars. An extraordinary amount of money for this place. It's their last purchase before they own this end of the beach, and they're willing to pay for it."

I couldn't even fathom that amount of money in our family. It made my head swirl. So did the fact that I was standing there with no undies on.

"OK, Marilen, let me think about it. I'll be in touch real soon, OK?"

She left with a nod. I shut the door firmly even though it was warm outside, blocking out the light from the beach. It was too much to think about. Not right now. Not with Tama's letter upstairs.

I ran up the stairs and tapped my phone. Google Translate offered an English word which shouldn't have surprised me: Shame. Why had Tama felt ashamed to be with me?

Now, my urge was turning primal, like an unnegotiable push of a uterus as a baby's head travels through it, like the drive for moisture against a parched tongue.

I grabbed Tama's note, the paua shell and the bird's feather and walked urgently to the backroom. My last full day in Maroa.

As I opened the door to my secret room, the smell softened whatever tensions I held in my neck. I took a step forward, fanning the edge of Tama's letter against my treasures on the high shelves. Heat seeped down my spine. I focused on the pin cushion I took from Grandma's sewing kit, nobbled pins bursting like starfish legs from its apple-shaped core. I touched a faded sock I'd picked up in a park in New York, Japanese emojis rimming the neck in bright oranges and greens.

I took another step forward, the letter dusting the lids of a row of jars, each with their own unique pattern and color – a stripe here, a pattern there. I remembered the lid collection I presented at the 4-H Club in Fifth Grade, where is that collection now?

I let myself go slowly towards the turn of the L-shaped room, taking in my possessions, first with my eyes, then my fingers, then my nose. Some of them filled my ears too. Does the wind-up plastic McDonald's toy from 1988 still make a sound? I closed my eyes and listened to its chink and fade, noticing how my thighs tightened as I remembered the first time I heard that song after kissing Matt Dawson in the McDonald's parking lot.

At the half-lit corner, I lay down on the floor, my torso and face capturing the light cast from the bulb, my lower half in the darkness of the shadows. My bare toes touched the bottom layers of my mound of treasures. I loved how my belongings seem to curve around my frame, hugging into me like a passionate embrace.

My fingers stroked the paua shell hard, then fell to my crotch. They moved up into its slippery folds as I moved the feather across my cheek with my other hand.

I lay there, completely absorbed in my surroundings, thrusting my feet further into the mound, touching and stroking my treasures, and letting the hours pass with no thoughts of rejection, of decisions, of loss, or even time.

Chapter 21

Upper North Island
Saturday, 29 October 2022

I half expected to see Tama walk along the beach as I put my suitcase into the rental car. A final kiss. A last-minute confession of love. But it was an ordinary departure, with the sound of the seagulls intermingling with the high voices of young children playing on the beach.

I took it all in – the smells, the way the light from the kitchen window landed on the old table, the latch of the door as I shut off my secret room. I tried not to think of this being the last time. If we sold this old place, I'd have to come back and pack up. Everything. I would move on.

Tama's letter was tucked safely next to the others in the shoebox with smiley-faced stickers. But the shell and the feather that he'd left me – they were packed carefully in my carry-on luggage. They'd be there for me if I needed them on the long flight home.

As I'd wiped the kitchen table for the last time, Marilen had rung to say goodbye, almost apologizing for coming off so strongly the day before. "It's just that I realize now how important your decision is, Cora. Not just to your family, but to the entire region."

I left mid-morning for my evening flight from Auckland airport. There was someone I wanted to see.

The winding drive back over the Coromandel Range took most of my attention; I still had to remind myself to drive on the left. I played Judas Priest while negotiating the hairpin turns in the road.

By the time I hit the wide motorway back to Auckland, I allowed myself to think about the past few days.

It was clear that EcoWorld needed me to agree to sell the property – and quickly. But would they go so far as to try to influence my decision by engaging with some of the people sitting next to me on planes? Would they actually prepare passengers or, darker still, pay actors pretending to be real passengers to convey particular messages to me?

And something else. Tama's note and sudden departure. He'd asked me upfront – so had Marilen – what I was planning to do with the bach. It seemed innocent at the time and, in that post-sex charm, I considered it to be natural conversation over fish and chips. Now I wondered if he, too, had been sent to scout out my intentions about the bach? Worse yet, had he enticed me into that intimacy *so* I would open up to him?

I shuttered the idea away. We had chemistry. There was no doubt he liked me and wanted to spend time with me; I was experienced enough to know the difference. But maybe he hadn't expected that. Maybe his mission to gather information from me turned out to be more than he could handle. "Whakama," or something.

I looked up at the clouds as I crested the Bombay Hills on the outskirts of Auckland. Like people, clouds are complex, interconnected systems that change and move according to the forces around them: heat, gravity, pressure. We compartmentalize them into tidy boxes: cumulus, humilis, stratus.

But seeing clouds in their scientific category is only one way of seeing them. Grandma had taught me not only their proper names, but also what they tell us about our world. And to remember to see them with a different set of eyes.

As I imagine the shape of a stooped witch as I fly past a towering cumulus, the boy in the row in front of me sees a moving ship, sails billowing and full. Both images are powerful and true. We impose our own pictures of meaning onto the trillions of water droplets that, at that moment in their incredible journey through the water cycle, have clumped together in a particular way.

Maybe our larger narratives are the same. Random interactions with people may be disconnected but can also be imagined as a linked-up story. In our lives of trillions of happenings, we connect the dots to make sense of things, to create patterns of meaning where there might in fact be none. Arbitrary. Accidental. Apophenia.

Maybe all those people I'd met on planes had no greater narrative; maybe they were just nice and on their own random journeys.

*

There were cute little vegetable stalls and cafes to stop at as I started to descend into greater Auckland. But I had to press on. There was an important stop to make before flying home.

Since Mom died, I always visited Aunty Rose during our trips to New Zealand. She wasn't my real aunt, but Grandma's best friend. In my childhood, Aunty Rose and Uncle Bobo would often be at the bach with us, forming part of the charm of the place, like the Formica table or the view from the kitchen window.

My child's mind stored a picture of Grandma and Aunty Rose toasting each other with glasses of wine and giggling naughtily as I emerged with Christopher at the top of the stairs, fresh from the beach. Each woman would take a child and throw a thirsty towel across our shoulders, rubbing wildly to warm us up, all while merrily complaining about the sand falling onto the carpet. Grandma and her friend laughed a lot in those years; it was something Aunty Rose recalled poignantly in her eulogy at Grandma's funeral, casting her blue eyes up as if her dear friend were up there, still laughing.

"Oh Ainslee," Rose had called to the ceiling of the old Anglican church in east Auckland, "even as the world around us changed, as people began to ignore us, even as – in *their* eyes – we became old women who had nothing to say, we still laughed, didn't we? We laughed when your daughter, Brona, was born. We laughed when she married an American called Bert. And then, when they called their own children names beginning with C's – Carl, Cora, Christopher – we laughed again. Your mokopuna, your grandbabies: Dylan and Dorothy. It seemed as if life was a story of alphabetized letters that kept being told, from one generation to the next … chapters of the story of your bloodline," and here, I remember Rose looking at me directly, "that the characters themselves didn't realize they were part of.

"Ainslee, you were the beginning of that story. But I know that your story and your legacy is far – at least 22 more letters in fact – from its end." And then Aunty Rose chuckled. We all sat in the cold church smiling through our tears.

Rose had outlived them all. With my mom and dad both dying at relatively young ages, I loved having an older connection to my New Zealand past. Like a homing pigeon returning to its roost, I always came back to visit her.

At 92, Aunty Rose was still sharp, chatty and rather unchanged from when I saw her three years ago. She waited for me in a soft chair in the expansive open lounge of the center. Dressed in a long skirt and sporty tennis shoes, she looked like she'd just come in from a walk. Her silver hair stroked her shoulders, framing her blue eyes like the streaks of falling water crowning the waterhole where I first met Tama.

I hugged her close. The decades of shared time and relationships held us together for a long moment. Would this be the last time? I asked that question with every visit, but she stayed strong and crisp, year after year.

"Look at you Cora! It's like looking at Ainslee all over again! You always were so like her. Sit down here next to me, dear."

"You're the youngest 92-year-old I've ever seen Aunty Rose! How do you do it?"

"Don't be silly, dear. I'm not that old!" She leaned forward and let her watery eyes sparkle. "Inside, I'm only 25!"

We laughed mischievously, holding each other's hands, in the memories of each other, in the memories of who we both used to be.

Our next words were about her health ("better than ever!"), her new hip ("it feels like a part of me now") and my restful holiday in Maroa Bay. To that, she said "you and that place always seemed to be pieces of a puzzle that fit perfectly together."

If I'd thought for a moment that I might let her know we'd likely have to sell the bach, I now knew that I simply didn't have the guts to tell her.

"Such wonderful times there," she continued. I saw her head nod repetitively, ever so slightly. I remember Sandra saying her own mother experienced hand tremors in her later years, to the point that she could no longer hold a glass on her own. "The upside-downness of your world reveals itself when you must hold a cup to your mother's lips, as she once did to your own," Sandra had said, poetically.

"And as I get older, Aunty Rose, I –"

"How old are you now, dear?"

"46"

"My goodness! You were just a pup a minute ago."

"And you – making that creamy dessert you always made with marshmallows and cream and – "

"Ambrosia."

"Yes ambrosia – man, I loved that stuff." In that moment I could feel it sliding down my teenage throat. One of the marshmallows may in fact even be molding in a corner of my special room. I shook off the idea as soon as it came.

"As I get older, I'm learning a bit more about the Coromandel area and its history and stuff. I guess I'd never really paid much attention to that sort of thing when I was younger."

"Oh yes, things of the past do become closer to our hearts as we get older," Rose smiled the same smile of at least 46 years.

"I met this guy from the area," I continued, "and he told me some of the old stories of the settlement and the early relationships between Māori and the settlers."

"Māori guy?"

"Yes, from the tribes around the Hauraki Gulf. I can't remember the names."

"Ngāti Pūkenga? Ngāti Rāhiri? Let's see, I think Ngāti Hako is from the area too."

I shouldn't have been surprised. Rose was a bit like Sandra, without the bad husband.

"Grandma always seemed interested in them. I remember her teaching us about the language and sometimes telling us some of the old stories too."

"Well, those things were always close to her heart."

"I'm starting to see why. The older I get, the more strongly I feel connected to that beach, that house, even the forests around it. It's hard to explain but, for me, it's moving into another level … an almost spiritual level."

The insight came even as I uttered the words. Rose shifted in her seat to more directly face me; I swiveled more towards her too.

"It was Ainslee's special place, you know, maybe even her people's place, the Coromandel."

"I know – she loved it. She called it her turangawaewae."

"Maybe it was." Rose's eyes became watery, and her gaze intensified. "Did she ever – did your Gran ever tell you that she was adopted?"

"Grandma? Not at all. Grandma?"

"She was, dear. She was two years old." Her voice was quiet and clear.

"Oh my gosh. I didn't know."

Aunty Rose looked to one corner of the large room, then nodded to herself. "She never knew her biological family. They didn't do that in those days. And to be honest, Ainslee wasn't really that interested in it – at first. But when she fell pregnant with your mum, it became more important to her. I guess some deeper connection to her past was triggered. And well, one of her theories is that she came from a Māori family."

"Māori? No way, she was Scottish, wasn't she?"

"Yes, she certainly looked like it with her reddish hair and fair skin. But a lot of Māori do have Scottish blood. Back then, the Government thought it was better for Māori kids to be raised in pākehā families. So, when families had problems or lots of other kids or a dad that went missing or something like that, they took Māori babies from their families and gave them to white couples with no children. It was common practice back then. Ainslee always wondered if she was one of them."

"What … you mean – wait – who were her family?"

"We never found out. But she'd always sensed that she came from the Coromandel. She believed, or maybe just imagined, that her family might be Māori."

I looked around the room, decorated as it was with formulaic artwork and interior upholsteries designed to convey cheer. I reached for my purse, plunging my hand into it.

"It was shameful, back then," Aunty Rose continued. "You see, people didn't talk about this stuff like they do now. These days, they're teaching it in schools and making everyone feel good about their ancestry. When Ainslee asked her adopted parents to tell her if her instincts were correct, they refused to say anything."

Her hand, thinned by years and lots of water, purpled with veins and oranged by ageing flesh, rested elegantly on her knee. I reached out for it, pulling my seat even closer. Rose clasped my fingers firmly.

"Your Gran loved Maroa Bay, and the fact that her people may've been from that area made it an even stronger pull for her. That's why she and your grandpa built a bach there."

I looked down at her hands in mine, squeezed them gently, then looked up at her face. It was so pure, almost angelic as she pressed her lips together in a soft, shaking smile. Time and laughter had carved deep lines there. I felt tears well as I imagined her gone from this world.

A deep voice interjected from above. "Rosey, who's this pretty lady?"

We looked up to see a wizard-like man beaming down at us. From his cheekbones to his hips, his hair to his wiry legs, he was a very sinuous man.

I didn't want our conversation to end. But the man's smile and flickering eyes commanded our full attention.

"Nigel!" Aunty Rose called out. "How lovely! This is Cora, my dear friend's daughter. Nearly one of my own."

I stood up to greet him, realizing he'd previously been a tall man that was now so stooped that it looked as if, above him, a low ceiling had to constantly be avoided.

We spoke to Nigel for a while – life on the lakeshore in Chicago, the mafia, the blues – and then, checking my phone, I announced I had a flight to catch. Nigel pulled away politely.

As I drew Aunty Rose close to say goodbye, I thought I could smell my summers at Maroa Bay in the silver curls behind her ears. In the absence of my mom and grandma, her muted, musky scent made me feel like that little girl again: alive, changing and part of something bigger than myself.

I kept my hands on her shoulders as we pulled away from each other. Her eyes rested on me calmly, studying my expression.

"Cora – are you happy with your life?" she asked.

I filled my chest with air, meeting her gaze. "Yes, I'm OK. It's just that - I have a lot of things to think about right now, including what you've just told me about Grandma. There's a lot – there's just a lot going on in my life."

The weight of my words made me pause. I willed the water in my eyes to not roll down my cheek. How could I end this moment on a more uplifting note?

"But I know that these experiences will make me stronger," I managed weakly.

"Strength is not happiness," she said. "But happiness does come from unexpected places."

We hugged again. Probably not for the last time.

*

It didn't really hit me until I stood in line at airport security. Grandma Ainslee, adopted? Could she have been Māori? Her people from that peninsula?

Wait, *our* people?

But she may've been wrong. Maybe it was her longing for a place of belonging after she found out she was adopted. Maybe she wanted to believe her biological family had lived for generations in the very place that she grew to love.

Did it matter? That she loved this place so intensely – isn't that enough?

I followed the line through the bag check and metal detector, then actioned my usual pre-flight bullet points: a snack (Air New Zealand dinner is a good three hours away), bathroom, phone.

There were five new messages since I'd last checked my phone, including one from Jess – *you back today?* – and one from Dottie.

I found a seat near the departure gate as the priority passengers stood up to board. There'd be just enough time to send the kids some photos of Maroa Bay before it was my turn to board. Two selfies, the house, the beach, with the caption "Paradise - but missed you so much! On way home with Pineapple Lumps!"

A male voice said "Air New Zealand flight 26 to Chicago now welcomes passengers in rows 42 to 60 to board the plane. Please present your boarding pass and your passport to Air New Zealand staff."

As I stood up, I realized I hadn't read Dottie's message. I shuffled into the line and looked at it quickly.

Mom - soz to tell u like this but I really want u to know before you get home. I'm pregnant.

I read the last word a second, then a third time. My hand clasped my throat, leaving my forearm to protect a deep, enclosed part of my heart.

"Ma'am?" said a uniformed woman with a tight hair bun and Tama's olive-shaped eyes, holding out her hand.

I showed her my documents. She thanked me and signaled me to walk down the boarding bridge. I looked again at the text, confirming, making sure I'd got the meaning right. I did that thing that I learned to do. Breathe. Think. Don't react immediately. Ask: what does she need right now?

At the bottle neck before boarding, the right words came. *Ok. Are you ok?* I typed. Her response was quicker than I'd expected. It was 1am in Chicago.

Actually, I'm great. Can't wait to see you and talk some more. Love you.

"Kia ora, welcome aboard. Just halfway down on the right," said a young man, with a quick glance at my boarding pass. His facial lines were clean, carved, crisp, c-. Stop it Cora.

The line inched forward. I read her message again. There was something soft there. Almost unrecognizable after so many years of depression. I let myself smile.

Love you too. I typed. Then added, *whatever you do, whoever you are, I will be there for you, no matter what.*

I pressed 'send' hoping my beautiful daughter, her verve and substance, her lithe and feminine body was lying in a fetal position under a warm comforter in the autumn night. I hoped she wouldn't see my text tonight, but was instead asleep, being loved and enshrined by whomever loved her at that moment in her life.

Typical of Dottie, her wishes didn't align with my own. She was awake and texted right back. *I know Mom. We've got this.*

As I settled into my window seat, different emotions began to well. Who is the father? How could she let this happen? This is life changing. Why hadn't I sent her to a different school before she got involved with that crowd and all those drugs? I could've made it work – we could've moved to the suburbs and gotten out of the city back then. Maybe I should've tracked down her father and sent her to live with Tom. God that's absurd Cora. It doesn't matter now.

Dottie is pregnant and wasn't expecting to be. She needs me. Maybe that would be a good thing for us right now. But if she goes ahead with the pregnancy, it's for a lifetime.

I needed a distraction. Soon, I thought whimsically, I would have to turn off my phone. I could enjoy 15 hours of mandatory connection-free time during the flight. Even when Dottie woke up, ready to talk and ready to argue, I would be thrusting at 600 miles an hour over the Pacific Ocean, ear-plugged and masked, dreaming of soft couches and horizontal mattresses, ready for non-airline coffee, ready to be clean.

No one came to sit in my row. The plane's doors were sealed. I couldn't believe my luck. The last time I'd had an empty seat next to me on a flight – much less two – seemed like never. Looking around, I could now see how lucky I was; there were only a few other empty seats in this section of the plane. Must've been a last minute cancellation.

As the voice on the speaker explained the flight's meal service and amenities, I realized I couldn't hide beneath a cloak of a Wi-Fi-free zone. This plane, the new Boeing 787, had endless Wi-Fi for passengers. If I wanted, I could stay connected all night. Invisible radio waves connecting with others, even thousands of miles out to sea. What capability: still mesmerizing. Even after all these flights.

I examined the tops of the cumulus nimbus shapes in the dusk above Auckland's Manukau Harbor, the artwork of unseen hands. It then occurred to me that Dottie didn't know about Air New Zealand's Wi-Fi on international flights. Last time she flew here, it wasn't available.

The plane tilted as it veered northwards, past the watery eyelids that had welcomed me to New Zealand's shores just a week ago, the blinking waves calling me home. Relaxed by the hum of the engines, I watched night creep in, casting ambers and lavenders across the cottony layer of clouds. Another day ended in front of my eyes, colorfully and gracefully, without thinking of Dottie, of Maroa, of Tama, of anything but clouds.

Above the world, I could detach. Only unimportant thoughts arrived: air friction, light refraction, and how complex these vast systems need to be before consciousness is achieved.

Dinner came. Tension in my shoulders drained down towards my feet. I let one arm and leg splay across the invisible line that separated my seat from the next one. A hot meal, a glass of pinot noir, the promise of not having to share the short row of seats with anyone else. I could even lie flat if I wanted. That mile-high sense of satisfaction – there must be a German or Japanese word for it – set in.

I was tempted to switch on a movie or podcast like everyone else on the plane. Or some Def Leppard. But now it was time – there was so much to think about.

Dottie. Maybe it's not a crisis. Where is the opportunity?

Grandma. What if her hunch were true? How could I find out? Could the New Zealand authorities reveal our family's history?

Had Mom ever been interested in, or even known, that her mother was adopted? Heading to college in the States at age 20, she may've been disinterested in her own ancestry. She was married to my dad just a couple years later, carving out an American life of her own. Maybe that's why it never came up when we visited her homeland during my childhood. Maybe, to Mom, her New Zealand past seemed even less relevant in her adopted culture.

And then there's the bach. An aggressive offer – EcoWorld had a lot at stake. Their offer of $3 million for a rundown old house was surprising, but it would bring a way out for Carl and Sandra, maybe even save their marriage. Easton Institute would be a real option for Christopher. If his results were like those of other clients, like the sister of that young woman I'd met on the plane, he could easily afford the transformative care from his portion of the proceeds of the family estate. And much more.

I could pay off the mortgage, finally renovate and sell my Lincoln Park property for a princely sum. Where would I go?

North Chicago? Maybe there would even be enough for the grander, tree-lined streets of Wilmette.

Dylan's university loan could be cleared in a minute, enabling him to get on with his life and invest in his future. Dottie, my god. Money would smooth the way for whatever path she chose. Abortion, adoption, solo parenting. I'd often thought I should send her to one of those career counsellors to work out, over several expensive sessions, how her interests align with a job. Or maybe I could simply pay her rent for a year while she nursed her newborn. Maybe it will never come to that. How would this change her? Change us?

Greece, a long-time dream. If I paid for Jess' flights, maybe they could afford some extra care for the girls while she was away.

There was something else I'd often thought about - Simon's boys. Isaac and Scott had always been special to me, and without a mom in their lives, I'd felt a certain responsibility to nurture them, to sustain. Even after Simon and I split up, this urge hadn't changed. Over the years, I'd thought about how they were doing, if they remembered me, and whether they could attract positive female relationships into their own lives after all they'd been through. From time to time, I googled their names or tried to find them on Facebook. Isaac had done well in football and seemed to be living in Arizona now. One photo showed him with a young child on his lap. Scott seemed to have no digital profile. I would love to see his 19-year-old face, aged by a decade since I'd said goodbye.

Over the years, I imagined reaching out to them in some way. A suggestion that I still cared and that, despite my failure to love their father, my affection towards them hadn't ended. And they knew Maroa Bay. Not long after Simon and I were married, they'd come to New Zealand with me – a sort of overseas experiment for our new family. It was, of course, an amazing holiday.

If we sold the Maroa house, I'd have good reason to reconnect, even sending them a small portion of the proceeds as a sign that in this small but symbolic way, I hoped to ease the pain that I may've caused them. Guilt money. Yes, that's probably what it was. But still. It's so hard to make your way financially as a young adult starting out in the world. I knew it would help.

Retirement savings. My neglect of it over many years would no longer matter. I could invest wisely, ensuring the comfortable, adventurous retirement I'd longed for. I could avoid the situation of the father whose son I'd met on a plane earlier this year; despite all that middle-class frugality, not much left in the end.

And my work, a year's salary could easily be skimmed off the profit from the sale. My own consultancy firm, my own hours, my own control. I felt my heart rate rise.

As I forked chicken casserole into my mouth with flared elbows and no concerns about disturbing anyone next to me, I couldn't believe that Grandpa's ramshackle holiday home could bring such profound and wonderful changes to the lives of his grandchildren, great-grandchildren, and soon enough, even his great-great grandchildren.

On the touch screen in front of me, I skimmed through the new releases, then the dramas. Nothing drew me in. I couldn't commit to 90 minutes of watching anything right now.

There was nothing but dark outside my window. The flight attendants cleared the dinner plates and dimmed the cabin lights. It had been an emotional and busy day; locking up the bach and farewelling the beach this morning now seemed as if it had been a week ago. I yawned and stretched out my legs across the three seats in my row.

I closed my eyes. There was so much to think about.

Chapter 22

AUCKLAND – CHICAGO (DIRECT)

DEPARTS 8.15 PM

29 OCTOBER, 2022

It was the smell of eggs that woke me up. Flight attendants moved down the aisles delivering special meals, leaning over passengers to hand hot breakfasts to children and vegetarians. I sat up, trying to shake off the terrible dream I'd been having: Dottie, swollen and red, being swarmed by flying, legged worms and buzzing insects. I watched her through the bars of a cage in the distance, powerless. Paralyzed. Pathetic.

I stood up and moved quickly to the line near the toilets, stretching my limbs as I walked. Not a bad sleep for an airplane. I still couldn't believe I had three seats to myself.

I made it back to my seat as the breakfast trolley appeared at the top of my section. Flicking at the on-board screen, I wondered if an old episode of "Friends" might go down well with a cooked breakfast.

A man sat down in the aisle seat of my row. At first, I thought he might be waiting there to get out of someone's way as they passed. When he looked straight at me, it occurred to me that his intentions might be directed my way.

His collared shirt was ironed under a smart-looking blazer. He must've slept in Premier Business on their flat beds to look that fresh. Of Chinese descent, his face was attractive and, though he was seated, his legs and torso were long and trim. He smiled at me, showing perfect, almost glaring, teeth.

"Good morning," he said gently. His voice was soothing and, I think, had an American accent.

"Good morning," I replied, with a questioning tilt of my head.

"My name is Andrew Chan. I'm from EcoWorld Resorts."

My chest tightened and my chin dropped. He flicked down the middle seat's tray. A cloth doily and two fluted glasses of something sparkling were placed on the tray. I glanced up at the face of the flight attendant – one I hadn't yet seen on this flight.

"Cora, allow me," he continued. Red heat climbed up my neck. What was happening?

"I've been looking forward to sharing this with you for a long time," he said, picking up a flute. "It is a Salon Blanc de Blancs Le Mesnil Brut, 2002," he announced in a learned French accent. "Simply exquisite."

I stared at him without moving as he sipped once, then closed his eyes and let out a satisfied breath. "Better than expected," he smiled.

"Who are you? How do you know my name – and seat number?" Inside my head I sounded shaken and weak, even as I tried to make my words sound more threatening to whoever this guy was.

He kept smiling like he knew something I didn't. I looked back two rows at the flight attendant, standing stiffly and looking straight ahead with a neutral expression on his face.

"Don't worry Cora," he said, "there's nothing to worry about. I'm only here to discuss a few things with you and I thought we could start our discussion with a little toast, that's all. But of course –" and then he lifted his right arm up slightly towards the aisle, which conjured up a small plate of fruit and miniature pastries to the tray table, "– you must be hungry after the long night. Please –" he signaled to the plate.

I sat speechless. Silent, staring, scared. The thumping of my heart was the only clue that I was alive.

At my motionlessness, he nodded slightly and continued. "Your family's owned the Maroa house for many years. I know how you've loved it. EcoWorld has worked closely with all the landowners along the beach, and with many others in the Coromandel region. But you, being so far away, it's been more difficult for us to discuss things with you directly. Please be assured, we've tried to contact you many times, but we understand how people don't often return calls to unknown numbers. Or emails for that matter," he blinked, suggesting I needn't apologize.

"So, we'd hoped the ABDA conference would better enable a face-to-face discussion."

The man took a sip of champagne and said, as if he was quite pleased with himself, "Ahh, so here we are, having a little chat!" He glanced up as the breakfast trolley parked near our row. A female flight attendant looked at him – did he nod at her ever so slightly? – before she asked the passengers in front of us if they wanted a cooked or continental breakfast.

"But now," he continued, "our organization is ready to take the next step and ensure the area can realize its full potential. Its beauty, its natural healing powers, its pure sea air – all of it will be able to be enjoyed not just by a few, but by the many who need it."

His American accent was educated and crisp. It sounded familiar and calming. I wanted to relax a bit more but – what did he just say about the conference in Australia? I looked at a plump grape on the tray table and felt more inspired to overcome my paralysis.

He continued. "Over the past few years, we've invested heavily into restoring the area's natural environment. Our donations have helped the bird sanctuaries and breeding programs lift several species, like the dotterel and the brown kiwi, from endangered to nearly thriving. We've helped rebuild infrastructure to move sewage safely out to sea instead of dumping it near the fragile ecosystems closer to shore. We've supported research on the area so scientists can better understand water quality and the microspecies that dwell there. We've nurtured the Coromandel Peninsula, as your own family has, for many years."

At this final statement, the man dropped his chin, closed his eyes and nodded slowly. I knew then that he'd been raised, despite his American accent, in an Asian household.

The flight attendant pushed the breakfast trolley past my row without even acknowledging me. I pushed a grape into my mouth.

"But unfortunately, our vision isn't understood by everyone who hears it, so we've had long delays in the Māori Land Court, and other bureaucratic hold-ups. Our window of opportunity to realize our dreams has taken an unforeseen turn, and now there's little time left."

He paused and, suddenly distracted, cast his eyes out the window. Dawn's first light struck through the window like a mole's nose emerging from its underground chamber. The unusual light held our gazes for a moment. An unexpected power.

He broke the spell with his voice. "Ahh, morning light … a promising sign of good fortune." He paused, then said, "Now, you are of course aware that we've made you a very generous offer for your place."

I nodded. Phonation was still not possible.

"Are you aware that every landowner in the development site has accepted our offers?"

I eyed the glass of fizzy. It was time to take a sip myself. The man waited patiently for me to respond. Wow – he was right. The bubbles were smooth.

"Yes," There was my voice. "Marilen, our property manager mentioned it," I said, trying to keep it light.

"Yes, she has," he said confidently. "And she has also mentioned a sum of money that we are willing to pay for your bach."

I nodded. Drank again.

"But you may not be aware, Cora, that both Carl and your husband agreed to the sale some time ago. We have the full support of your family's trust members, except for yours. And of course, Christopher's."

So many things made me bristle. Hearing my brothers' names spoken by this stranger. The word "husband" – I hadn't considered I'd had one anymore. And Christopher – I suddenly remembered I hadn't spoken to him this week even after Dylan said he needed to get in touch.

"Cora, just before I stepped onto this flight, I received approval from the EcoWorld board to leave you with a new figure that we're willing to, after much deliberation, pay your family for your place. You'll see that it's *very* generous and far above what we'd normally pay for such a small parcel of land.

But it represents our understanding of how special the old bach is to you and ..." he paused and looked straight at me, "the special memories it houses."

I returned his stare, feigning confidence. How could he know about my special room? Not even my family talks about it. Maybe Marilen had had a key made. Carl – surely, he didn't care or even remember. Bryce and Simon had only been there once each, and I'd made sure as hell they didn't suspect a thing.

"And I urge you," the man continued, "to remember two things as you consider our very gracious offer. EcoWorld has and will continue to make the Coromandel a better place for all its inhabitants, whether plant, animal, or human.

"And with our new resort, millions more will go into sustainable projects that will make the area thrive for generations to come. We'll build roads and schools, water treatment plants and marae for the Māori people. That's our vision. And secondly – "

"Wait," I said, "do you mean just the hotel on Maroa beach?"

"That is the first of many major projects we have underway on the Peninsula. Once the Maroa resort is completed, we can better demonstrate the benefits we're having in the region. Our vision is long-term and located across many sites. But first, our focus is on Maroa Bay."

I could no longer resist the miniature chaussons aux pommes from the breakfast plate, plucking one with slightly shaking fingers.

"And secondly, I hope that you can fully imagine the changes you can now make in your life with this sale: help for your family members, a comfortable retirement, trips around the world … these things will all be within your reach. No more worries about your responsibilities, a clear pathway to success for your children."

I emptied my flute and, as I placed it on the table tray, a hand appeared above it, holding a bottle. My glass was full again and the man carefully placed an embossed envelope on the tray table between us.

"Cora, our single, non-negotiable, and final offer must be accepted in the next two days. After this, our window of opportunity to execute our plans will close. I'm sure you'll do the right thing for both your family and the people of the Coromandel. My contact details are in the envelope."

The man bowed his head once, slow blinking, cat-like. "It's been a pleasure to meet with you," he said, then stood and took quick, long strides towards the front of the plane. A hand reached down to lift his empty flute. The doily was left behind. As quickly as they'd arrived, they were – both the man and the arm from above – gone.

Breathe. Two three.

I looked around to see if anyone else had taken notice of the oddity of this visit, but all the passengers were eating breakfasts, plugged into their headsets and staring at their screens. The flight attendants rattled dishes behind me in the service kitchen. I sunk back into my seat and pleaded to the clouds for comfort.

Far below, they quickly changed from shimmering gold to orange-tipped as the morning sun bounced off their tops.

I took in another mouthful of champagne and examined the decorated envelope. Fingers of possibilities reached out to me. The solution to so many problems in my life, to Carl's, to Christopher's, could be inside that envelope. It was sealed with wax, old school. I broke the seal with a quiet snap. The paper was soft and finely textured. I slid the paper from the envelope and unfolded it.

I quickly scanned words like "EcoWorld International Ltd graciously offers" and "please accept." but it was the figure at the bottom of the page that my eyes landed on. The curve in the lower part of the number seemed to smile at me, like a hostess welcoming me into the Business Premier class of a plane.

Now, the thick woolen layer of cumulonimbus shielded the Pacific Ocean from my view, but the ombre colors above it reminded me of the ever-moving sea. Layer upon layer of orangey pink, then pinky orange, melted into the next, each layer darker as it moved away from the sun.

A new sensation rested in my chest. I listened to the plane's engines for a moment then looked down at the figure again.

US $5 million. That unnerving man had been right. This could certainly change things.

Chapter 23

*Maroa Bay
Saturday, 7 January 2023*

Here we are, drawn together in this place, like so many years before.

I wonder what we look like from above, bouncing like water particles towards and away from each other, clustering then de-clustering as we stand barefoot on the sand.

They're all here. My people. Him too. I can't believe he's here.

Dottie's hands linger under her belly. She strokes, then holds, strokes, then rocks. Her father places a curved hand on her shoulder.

"Let me try," he says. "'Mokopuna' – is that right Cora? My grandchild. I can't believe I'm old enough to say that!" Dottie moves Tom's hand to her abdomen, her wide smile dominating her face. I see her eight-year-old self, now shaped by a new power.

"That's right – mokopuna," I say. Breathe Cora. Not too fast. I look at Tom and then down to the boulders at the other end of the beach. We danced there, in the rain, once.

"There's a lotta years to make up Dottie," says Tom and then he pauses, as if waiting for something. "But I'll be there … I'll be there."

"So will I," says Dylan, bursting into our group. Janey squeezes in next to him. "We've got this, eh sis?"

"We'd better, *Uncle* Dylan," she laughs, which seems to sway her body back and forth, forth then back.

Dylan pulls Janey and Dottie into a huddle, and they whisper playfully, leaving Tom and I to stand like two pelicans pointing our beaks to the sand. He touches my arm, and we step away from our children, saying nothing. His look is empathetic. Easy. Emotionally available.

My two brothers and Sandra appear at the garage door with a pitcher of something icy. Tom and I watch them walk towards us, a comfortable silence sitting between us.

"Who needs a top-up?" Carl lifts the jug of something yellow-green into the air. Dylan pushes his glass towards his uncle.

Christopher is freshly showered from the long flight and wears a floral short-sleeved shirt that I've never seen before. I do all his shopping. This is an interesting development.

He walks straight to Dylan and says with unchecked enthusiasm, "I paid for everything myself! Do you like it?"

"Awesome Uncle Chris. You're looking snatched."

"I know! I earn so much money now."

"How's the new job going anyway? Do you like it?"

"It's a real job like you and Carl. I wear a uniform and there's a lady who stands across from me who's real nice. Sarah. She's not as fast as I am at packing. But she talks to me. We're going to see Elvis in concert!"

Everyone around him laughs and Dylan pats Christopher's back, asking about the concert.

I think of Mom and Dad and blink my eyes to sweep away the moisture. I look at Carl, who's already looking at me. He nods, ever so slightly. I look out to the waves which, like the memories of our parents, come and go, but are always there. I hear the voice of Grandma calling from the bach *is a big person with you Cora?*

I turn back to Tom, who's waiting for me, ready.

*

"I guess you want to know what happened – with this place, with all the dramas," I said, knowing there's so much I don't want to admit. "What have the kids told you?"

"Not much," Tom said. "Talking about you with them is kinda outa my league – like talking about 'the war' or something."

I watch the lines around his eyes deepen as he smiles. Whatever hardships the years have handed him, he hadn't lost the softness of his expression. "They said something about the people who sat next to you on your work trips had something to do with it."

I shrug my shoulders. "It wasn't every flight I went on, but every few weeks I'd find myself chatting to someone where it felt like they were speaking directly to my life – like they knew more about me than any stranger should.

"I remember one day, standing in line for the restroom on a flight and wondering: can that guy who wants to talk about business' environmental impacts or something be for real? Or is something else going on? Then when I started thinking back, there must've been three, or maybe even more other flights where there were these people sitting next to me who were just unusually keen on talking."

Tom shakes his head slowly.

"Sometimes, my thoughts sounded totally paranoid to me – like I was going mad imagining these strangers having some hidden motive. But – you know how I can tend to catastrophize – so I was trying to stop myself from doing that by just ignoring the signs that were sitting right next to me."

"You always were pretty easy to talk to. But that is nuts."

"I tried to put the idea of some sort of collaborated scheme out of my head. It seemed so far-fetched. But when I got here to Maroa Bay in October, that's when it became clear that

EcoWorld had a massive plan to build a resort not only right here on this beach, but on beaches throughout the Coromandel. They're a huge international company that's been investing here for a long time – they have squillions of dollars to put into realizing their plan."

A squeal comes from Dottie behind us. Dylan and Janey high-five her and Dottie teases her brother "Does she *actually* know what she's getting into? I mean, you're not exactly an uncomplicated guy."

"I'm sure you'll let her know," he kisses Janey on the cheek. Dottie beams at them both.

"Looks like they're scheming too," says Tom, out of one corner of his mouth. We watch them for a moment. I notice Dylan's jawbone hardening in the frame of his handsome face as he talks. It reminds me of, back then, watching Tom over the shoulders of our friends in a noisy bar or a bowling alley. I'd watch his jaw get squarer and his eyes brighten, and I used to think: I love that and I want to give that to the kids we make together.

Not long after, we did.

"So, they offered you some of their squillions while you were here?"

"Yep, and I was tempted, of course. *Sorely* tempted. It was a lot of money – what those dollars could mean for Christopher and the kids. And –" I watch my older brother sweep an arm around his wife's waist. "And with what Carl and Sandra are going through, I had to think long and hard about what it could mean for all of us."

"I'll bet."

"But –" I fling my palms outwards, looking to both ends of the beach. "How could I let go of this beach, our history here … you know? Especially after what I learned about Grandma. What if she really were indigenous here? Even if she weren't, it feels important to me that she connected so strongly to this place."

I hear my voice lift in pitch. "So I told EcoWorld 'no' and that no matter how much they offered me, it'd always be 'no.'"

I reach into the pocket of my shorts for something to stroke. The necklace I'd found underneath the seat of the rental car isn't there; it must still be in my purse. I breathe in, then out.

Then, I look out to the ancient headlands and the boulders at the ends of the beach and the waves of saltwater that have always healed my cuts and sorrows. Then I look to my people, my clan, my Dunbar's inner circle of eight.

Here, with them: this is enough.

"Hopefully," I say to Tom with fresh vigor, "our kids will make the same decision in the years to come."

Tom brings his fingertips to my forearm. Energy – deep and old and new – passes between us. I take it in and let it move around inside me.

"Anyway," I continue after a few moments, "As soon as I found out who was in cahoots with EcoWorld, I couldn't fucking believe it."

I'd been foggy and tired when I'd come into the office the morning after my flight from New Zealand. Arlene had said "Girl, when you gonna stop being the star of the show 'round here? Seems like you gotta few things to talk to Steve about."

I'd thought she'd meant that feedback from the Australian conference had come through. But a few moments later, Steve informed me that there'd been a "serious breach of privacy." Greg, our web guy, had been sending my travel plans, including seat numbers, to "third parties outside of our firm's security wall."

It was only a little ironic that Steve's tie that day had little pictures of flashlights on it, some off, some on, shining a light into the darkness.

"Do you know someone named Bryce Edwards?" Steve had asked, innocent and somewhat pale-faced.

I'd looked down to my feet and wished I'd brought my purse into his office with me. All I could utter were two words. "My ex."

"I filed for divorce as soon as I could," I tell Tom on Maroa beach. "I should've done it as soon as he'd left."

"What was he thinking?"

"Illinois state law honors the common law marriage terms of other states, including Iowa – that's where we got married.

So, he was entitled to half of my portion of the sale of the bach."

"When did you split up?"

"Well, technically we hadn't. I got up one day and he was gone. Left a farewell note on the kitchen table and just disappeared from my life. Kind of like – "

I stop myself. Tom's face darkens and he averts his eyes to the sand. I didn't need to say that. Not today anyway.

The sea breeze pulls back my hair and I lower my voice and lean closer to him, speaking to his forehead. "When he left me, it shook every fiber in my body, every nerve ending I had left. I just switched everything off. It was the only way to keep going."

I raise the pitch of my voice. "When EcoWorld tried contacting me about the sale of the bach and couldn't get through, well, when I didn't return their overseas calls, they tracked Bryce down from our marriage certificate. He was quite obliging to share plenty of information about my life to get me to sell."

"Like what?"

"Christopher, my love of different cultures, not being able to save for retirement, stuff like that."

Tom leans toward me further. "I'm sorry for you, Cora. I wanted you to find someone that made you happy. You raised our beautiful kids alone and I just –" He looks out to the waves as if to find more words there.

"I'm sorry," he mouths, his eyes holding mine.

It may not ever be enough, but there is nothing more to say, for now.

*

A deep laugh comes from the top of the beach. The colors of Marilen appear like an erupting sunflower against the monochrome of the sand. She clutches red garden flowers and wears a bright orange hat. It seems like last week that we sat in Grandpa's lawn chairs right here and drank gin together.

She hugs Carl, then Christopher and congratulates Dottie on her new shape.

As she pulls me into a hug, she says "I'm so sorry to hear of Aunty Rose. My mum adored her."

I nod, holding back my tears. Tom touches the skin between my shoulder blades and presses it gently.

"You certainly put in motion some big changes around here, girl!" Marilen's laugh stops Christopher talking for a moment. "Let's catch up after you all settle in. How's the bach – everyone fitting in OK?"

"Of course! Grandma and Grandpa designed it like that, didn't they?! It's perfect."

Marilen turns to Tom and raises her eyebrows. I say "Remember Tom? He used to come here with us some 15, 20 years ago. I'm not sure if you were around here then, but – "

"Auckland," Marilen says. "Lived there till 2007 before I realized I was missing out on my family's little bit of paradise out here. Nice to meet you, Tom!" I see her eyelids blink a little more quickly than usual as she makes small talk with him. I resist the urge to reach out and grab Tom's hand.

Marilen soon makes a beeline for Carl and Sandra. Sandra heads towards the bach to get a glass for her.

We shift towards our kids and Janey and Christopher. Tom spreads his arms to surround Dylan and Dottie. I guess I'm a little surprised at how comfortable he's become in their presence, as if he hadn't missed the making of them. A bookmark never lost.

I ask Dottie: "Are there any baby names you like that begin with E? You know you have a bit of a legacy to carry on …"

"Evelyn?" says Dylan.

"Elliott?" offers Tom.

"Elvis!" shouts Christopher. We all crack up.

Behind me, I hear Marilen saying to Carl "– and by Cora turning down their offer, all sorts of other EcoWorld plans failed too." I keep my back to them, listening.

"But it seems to have inspired other districts to challenge their land buy-ups right across the Coromandel. They'd been quietly working for so long in the background that, when this story hit the papers here, everyone seemed to wake up from their dream state and see what EcoWorld was trying to do. It's no wonder, even *I* started going down that rabbit hole of what they could offer to these little communities.

"Thank goodness a reporter got her hands on their long-term strategy and, bloody hell, let's just say it had nothing to do with being 'Eco' and everything to do with 'World'... domination, if you know what I'm saying!" Marilen cackles.

I turn to face them, as Sandra offers a plastic glass and Carl tips liquid into it. In Marilen's blossoming cheeks and her eyes, I now see relief.

"So the whole thing," she continues as she nods at me, "has finally got the central government to notice how tempting these types of public-private partnerships are for us locals. They've stepped in, so there's already talk of two new schools and a bigger sewage treatment plant. One of the local Māori tribes has just settled their Treaty of Waitangi land claim and they're looking at investing into more accommodation and social services too. The area is gearing up for a big boost in public funding."

"Maybe that's why the Townsends," says Carl, "you know the ones next to us, are wanting to increase the size of their section. They've approached us about buying some of our back section, near the driveway. Sounds like the residents here want to build things up too."

"True!" Marilen says. "It feels like there's a lot of optimism here right now. You should get a pretty penny or two for that little clip of land, Carl, with it being right here on the beach and all."

"Yeah," he says. "That'll help."

Sandra touches the back of Carl's arm. It's the first time I've seen them both together since Carl's mistakes caught up with him a few months ago, except in O'Hare airport before we all boarded.

I'd enjoyed talking to Carl more regularly since then, even if it was largely about how I could help him and Sandra repay his enormous debt. Because talking about the family's finances often led to conversations that had nothing at all to do with money. Like his fondness for my kids. Like his insecurity about his success as a man, despite his confident veneer. Like coming on this trip together, again. And at last.

I admire Sandra's understated beauty as she takes in Marilen's words, silently touching her husband. I see something stronger, longer, lashing them together.

Marilen tips the last of the liquid out of her glass and says something about having to be somewhere. As we hug again, she says, albeit a little too loudly, "What a brave thing you did, Cora. You nailed shut a door that should've never been opened."

We pull back from each other, holding hands loosely. Her freckled skin strikes out from the backdrop of her orange hat, like a peak of sunshine through a cloud. Like, well, a daisy.

"Let me know when you're next in town for a gin or a scone," she says.

"You'll be the first to know," I say.

As Marilen marches up towards the road, the shape of our group changes again. Carl shifts towards Tom and the kids, leaving Sandra and I moving towards one another; the sister, I now see, that I never had.

"How'd it go with Steve after all that?" she asks. "Did he finally give in?"

"That massive breach of privacy helped. Once I told him that there wouldn't be any legal action from me against his firm, the funds for a new full-time position miraculously appeared. I've got another trainer starting next week!"

"Thank goodness huh?" she says.

"If he only knew how close I was to throwing in the towel."

"My god, Cora, what are you going to do without so many frequent flyer points and hotel rooms and corporate lounges and –"

"Live my own life!" I say, almost shouting.

Sandra and I talk about Christmas with her family and her choir's holiday performance. I tell her about how my first Christmas cards to Isaac and Scott were met with enthusiastic emails from both of them. Scott said he remembers my "warm, juicy hugs and great cooking," and hinted that his dad, Simon, had happily re-married.

"See? You're still in their hearts, Cora. And I know they're still very much in yours."

"Thanks. That means a lot to me." I look across the beach to see the 9-year-old Scott grimacing as the Maroa waves smack his belly.

"How are things going with Carl?"

"Better," she says. "We're starting to see a way out. You've been terrific throughout this whole, nasty affair."

My feet sink further into the soft, summer sand. Today, I don't imagine a cavern opening up underneath them. I stand there, feeling strong and solid. My place to stand.

Sandra and I turn our shoulders towards the rest of our family, all in various stages of conversations. Christopher and Dylan are poking fun at each other about the new haircuts they both had before this trip. Janey and Dottie are deep in conversation with their arms folded over their chests, importantly. Carl and Tom talk loudly to each other as if they hadn't just spent 16 years apart, living completely disparate lives as a banker and an alcoholic.

I was reminded briefly of Carl's comments when I first brought Tom home to meet our family back in our 20s.

After Tom left, Carl had said understatedly, "He'll do" with a rare nod of his head.

Back then, that, and my newly enriched sex life, was all that I needed to take my relationship with Tom to its next stage.

Carl tips more of the drink into my glass, winking at me.

I ask Tom to get people's attention, so he picks up a stone and clinks it against his glass. Everyone turns to face us.

I look down at my white toes against the sand, like cumulonimbus growing in front of a darkening sky.

"I can't really explain what it means to me, and probably Carl and Christopher too, to have you all here with us, in this place. It has to do with our connections to each other and to those ancient boulders over there, and the woods beyond them. And the waves. It's just – "

I breathe in. Two. Three. Then out.

"When we're at Aunty Rose's funeral, I hope you take notice of the ways in which the people that knew her talk about her life. Listen to their stories. Dottie, Dylan - you were far too young when our parents died, your grandma and grandpa."

Even Christopher is still. From here, he looks rounded, his face mature and full.

I turn to my kids. "I know it's hard for you to appreciate, but here, on this beach, it's where many of these connections happened, and it's where we have a real reason to explore and make sense of who we are. Maybe you'll hear things at the funeral that help you better understand the story of you. And a part of that story is right here, in Maroa Bay."

Dottie's shoulders rise as her hands encircle her belly. Dylan casts both his arms around her and Janey.

The moment is quiet. Impregnated. Filled with the invisible energy of clouds.

Then Christopher shouts "Cora, you're like Mom, but different."

Everyone laughs.

Christopher. My Christopher.

Dylan's voice lifts above the chatter.

"And because this place is so special to us," he says confidently, "Janey and I are planning to have our wedding right here on this beach. Same time, next year."

Our cheers and claps sweep down the beach – I see a group of beachcombers look our way. We hug and pat and congratulate and tease and as I pull in my beautiful boy, he says, "Is that OK, Mom? Can we have it here?"

I hold his shoulders in both my hands and look up at the house, its cracked garage door, the peeling paint. Janey's family is big, and quite well-off. Where would they all sleep?

"Absolutely. There're some family traditions to carry on," I said, beaming with the pride of generations. "Now, tell me everything! How did you ask her? Where were you? Was it a surprise?"

Everyone huddles around Dylan and Janey. Tom reaches for my hand. I grab Christopher's with my other.

Above us, the clouds drift towards the hills.

Interstice

Above Maroa Bay
7 January 2023

High in the earth's atmosphere super saturated air collides with particles of dust to form ice crystals If the temperature and moisture are right a snowflake is formed growing as it travels through the sky attracting more moisture more dust Trillions of snowflakes move in unison to form powerful systems that can cause unspeakable devastation or immense joy

These powers belie the quiet joining of particles of dust and air that give birth to it Forces that are hidden and miniscule can grow into the greatest of energies

Now Sky-facer stops at the door and looks down at the cracked step Her shoulders straighten She turns back to the beach to its southernmost end Her head jerks up to the drive and then the dirt road and then the beach carpark

She bends down to lift a paua shell in one hand and in the other a feather of a Tūī as it is known to the first people of this land

Sky-facer holds both items carefully then moves them slightly to watch their iridescence of blues and purples as they shift in the sun's light With a hopeful look she surveys the beach ... waits ... looks to the road ... then moves inside

As we drift inland we see her in the upstairs window through ill-fitting curtains She draws away from the window and slips into the darkness of another room as if sucked by a great force

Then we are pulled apart to become something else Something new

Acknowledgements

A novel is somewhat of a cloud. It attracts and becomes something different because of the incredible forces around it.

My first readers Michelle, Haidee, Sal, Helen, Coraller of Notes Amanda and Eagle-eyed Katie – you inspired the shifts that needed to happen. Second readers Lisa and Kate (who had been exposed to some of my quirky molecules) and third readers Maria, Anne, Gail, Jenny, Frances, Jan and Bea (who hadn't) – your generosities of insight and detail had the uplift of a towering cumulus. Swirling around again came Bea, Jo and Katie with their formidable powers.

Editor Michelle Elvy, whose circumnavigation of the planet by the power of wind, twice, must've made her re-thinking of how this story could be told seem easy. Thank you for the big and little reframes that brought the structure and revealing to a better light.

The force of external momentum cannot be understated in a 7-year project. There are too many to mention here, but you are the ones that asked, listened, provided writing sanctuaries, and trusted that this would come to light. Thank you for the many ways that you helped keep it all afloat over many years.

For most of their remembered childhoods, Fynn and Jade knew that, while dinner was being cooked, cats fed, and homework done, I'd slip away to my office to write, edit and market this story. Thank you both, and Gemma, for giving me the time to untrap Cora from her lashings. Your independence, confidence, and besotted love of your father's cooking gave the story room to gather.

Andrew, your mountaineer's stamina reaches into every aspect of our lives, even when mine flounders. Thanks for it all. Let's go sailing.

www.ingramcontent.com/pod-product-compliance
Lightning Source LLC
Chambersburg PA
CBHW020340010526
44119CB00048B/533